Betting on Flat Handicaps

Jon Gibby

ACKNOWLEDGEMENTS

I would like to express my thanks to my family for their encouragement and support and particularly to my parents who gave me a racing education. They taught me to count: Nine to four, one hundred to thirty, eleven to two ... and while other kids were taught that a yankee was an inhabitant of one of the northern states of the USA and that a double was a measure of alcohol, my parents introduced me early on to the real meanings of these words!

Thank you to Stuart for persuading me to go ahead and write this book.

A special thank you to my wife Helen and my boys James and Owen for their support and understanding even though they must have been heartily sick of finding me hunched over a computer keyboard for much of 2001 when there were so many better things I could have been doing!

Many thanks to Raceform for allowing me to produce this book under their banner.

Published in 2002
by Raceform Ltd
Compton, Newbury, Berkshire, RG20 6NL
Raceform Ltd is a wholly owned subsidiary of MGN Ltd

A Catalogue record of this book is available in the British Library.

ISBN 1-901100-29-4

Designed by Sam Pentin
Printed by Bookcraft, Midsomer Norton

Contents

INTRODUCTION

The majority of people I know have no interest in horseracing and I suspect that most of them consider it to be a dubious and dangerous pursuit, having been warned off as youngsters by their grandparents continually repeating that old mantra: 'you can't beat the bookie'. Occasionally some unsuspecting souls have made the mistake of showing a glimmer of interest in the subject and have been rewarded by me bombarding them with a seemingly endless hail of explanation, statistics and ideas. They try to look receptive but it is usually not long before their eyes glaze over and the shutters come down.

The fact is, to the uninitiated, horseracing is a total bore! It frustrates me that so few people I know want to discuss the subject, but there is no use me trying to find a soul mate in my local betting shop because most of them are simply beyond caring! Hence this book. As I am unable to talk to anyone about racing I have written about it in the hope that someone out there might be interested!

FIRST BETS

On a recent trip to my parents' house I was looking through the contents of the wardrobe in my old bedroom when I discovered two yellow exercise books. Curious, I dusted down the cover of the top one and revealed the legend *NEW SYSTEM 1984*. Recognising my handwriting I turned to the first page to discover that it contained a list of 18 bets. The other pages were blank. I cannot recall the rules of that particular system but it started well enough, finding a couple of short-priced winners and showing a modest profit before seven consecutive losers left it a couple of points in deficit. It seems I was unable to deal with this disappointment and that the system was unceremoniously dumped.

On examining the other book I was amused to discover it too was endorsed *NEW SYSTEM 1984*! Any record of my bets had to be testament to my betting prowess, not my failings, and I had obviously moved quickly onto another book in an effort to expunge that initial failure! On opening the second one I found that the first page contained the details of only eleven selections which had returned a loss. The other pages were blank!

We all probably fit the description 'mug punter' when we first begin betting and this discovery reminded me that I was certainly no different! I had no idea what I was doing in those days and in common with a lot of novice punters my lack of know-how led me to seek the refuge of systems. There is something attractive about systems to the insecure punter whose limited knowledge and experience means that he has little confidence in his ability to interpret form.

Systems lend a comforting structure to the selection process and they do away with the difficulty of evaluating past performances and taking decisions. Furthermore, when things inevitably go wrong it is easier for the system user to come to terms with his failure, because he can lay the blame on the inadequacies of the system rather than himself. He can cope with a system failing because he still has the dream that in time he will discover a winning formula!

THE NEED TO SPECIALISE

In common with most punters who rely on systems, I lost. In those days I had no concept of value and I wrongly believed that the route to success was to pick as many winners as possible. My systems were painfully unimaginative and each one differed only by the emphasis I placed on the various factors I considered to be important.

I was hampered by my belief that where horses finished in relation to each other in a race, how much weight they carried and how much weight they subsequently carried, were the most important factors influencing the outcome of a race. My systems were designed to select a horse that ideally had the best recent form, the best trainer, the best jockey and had conditions in its favour. They picked their fair share of winners but the prices were too short for a profit to be realised because in common with many system users I was taking the most obvious factors into account and my selections were entirely unoriginal. I believed that the reason for my failure was that I was not picking enough winners and I wasted my time tinkering with the weighting I gave to the various factors in an attempt to find a system that picked more.

I stumbled along in this way for some time, experiencing little success, and it was not until I finally took the decision to dispense with systems and to specialise in sprint handicaps in 1990 that my betting began to noticeably improve. I soon realised just how important it is to get to know a particular group of horses well. How having more knowledge of their likes and dislikes gave me an edge over those punters who only scratch the surface of races because they cast their nets too wide in search of winners.

I also started to appreciate the powerful impact that the draw has on the outcome of many sprint races. After deciding to concentrate on well-drawn runners, I found that I was able to highlight horses at long odds that were likely to run into a place or win. For the first time I found a way of picking outsiders that had a realistic chance of winning and I enjoyed a good measure of success from each way betting. However, my knowledge of draw bias was still basic and as I was not producing my own figures I had to rely on the limited and often wrong information that was available in the press!

In 1992 Nick Mordin's book *Betting For a Living* was published. Although Mordin had drawn a lot of his inspiration from the works of American racing authors, his book was nevertheless a revelation for punters like me who had had to make do with the banal offerings from other British writers. These writers preferred to glorify racing's heroes such as Red Rum and Lester Piggott rather than offer anything constructive on the subject of form analysis. It was this book that introduced me to things that had long been understood on the other side of the Atlantic, such as the importance of pace, class, the physical appearance of horses and performance patterns. It also provided me with some very useful pointers on how to produce draw figures. And perhaps most importantly it made me realise that there was a lot to learn from the extensive writings of American authors such as Andrew Beyer, Tom Ainslee and William Quirin, whose existence had up to that point escaped me!

Having been inspired by Mordin I read some of the American works that he had advocated and I was impressed. Some of the authors had excellent academic credentials and their well-written and well-researched material proved that the subjects of form study and betting do respond well to intellectual analysis and are not purely speculative. Although I found most of what I read persuasive I was aware that, due to their pari-mutuels and the fact that their tracks are predominantly dirt, American racing is quite different to ours and I was doubtful whether the ideas I read about could be successfully applied in the UK. There was only one way to find out, so I set about the task of researching the matter. After seemingly endless hours of hard work ploughing through old form books I was relieved to discover that I had not been wasting my time; most of what I had read about was equally valid to our racing.

After putting my research to the test I decided to concentrate my efforts on handicap races because I felt the American-style approach I was developing would be seen to best advantage in these races. After all, the levelling effect of weight means that the ability of each horse is not as important an issue as it is in non-handicaps and it is common for handicaps to be determined by factors such as the draw, class and pace, rather than the ability of the runners. In non-handicaps, without the effect of weight the best horses can win irrespective of these other factors, because their influence is often marginal and is decisive in determining the outcome of a race only when the abilities of the horses are closely matched.

This decision to concentrate on handicaps and the effects of bias significantly improved the profitability of my betting and over the last few seasons I have become convinced of the merits of the approach that I have adopted. During the 2000 Flat season I made a level stakes profit of 134 points and the approach highlighted a good number of long-priced winning bets and yet maintained a decent strike rate. This book will show you how this level of profit was achieved in practice.

Of course I realise that there are numerous ways to make a profit from betting on horses and it is not my intention to try to persuade you that I have found the truth, the whole truth and nothing but the truth! Yes, I have developed a profitable method but I recognise that its prosperity may be of a transient nature. Inevitably, the quality of the information available to punters about bias will continue to improve and it will become tougher to maintain an edge over the competition. I accept that this state of affairs calls for a fluidity of approach and that I will need to continue to try and find new ways of moving my betting forward. Notwithstanding this, I hope that you find some of the ideas in this book fresh and interesting and that they challenge at least some of the preconceptions you may have.

NO SHORT CUT TO SUCCESS

It took me years and endless hours of research and analysis to obtain the knowledge and experience I needed to become a decent punter. Although short cuts to success in this game are rarer than a professional footballer with a degree, I suppose the object of this book is to help you reach that same goal in a shorter period of time. Although it contains the information necessary for you to improve your betting, I admit that I doubt whether it is possible to short cut the time required to learn the mental discipline that is needed to successfully apply the information, particularly if you are a relative newcomer to the game.

The greatest hurdle facing you is not a lack of knowledge, because that can be acquired reasonably quickly, but a lack of discipline. I could bore you with pages of psychobabble about the difference between winners and losers but I do not believe there is any point for you cannot learn mental discipline by reading a book.

It took several years of unpalatable losses to persuade me to change my ways and to become more disciplined and I suspect that you will have to go through a similar experience. For those of you who have already been on that learning curve but are still losing, I am confident that this book will be a significant help in your quest to realise a profit!

The book attempts to persuade you of the need to think and act differently to other punters and it examines how I endeavour to achieve this in practice. It takes a detailed look at the subjects of pace, class and the draw and explains how they and other biases can be used to narrow a field of handicappers down to its logical contenders. It then looks at ways to determine which of the contenders are about to produce their best form and how to decide between them. And finally the last chapter illustrates how the theory works in practice.

Whether you are persuaded by the merits of the approach or not, the comprehensive draw and pace charts contained in the book ought to be of significant value to you, irrespective of the selection method you employ.

CHAPTER ONE

THE IMPORTANCE OF BEING DIFFERENT

In his book *Betting For a Living* Nick Mordin provided a clue as to why most punters fail to make money from betting when he wrote: 'Forget any fantasies you may have about betting every winner on the card. You will have to accept that the way to win more money involves backing a greater percentage of losers. This is perhaps the biggest challenge of all facing you as a would-be professional gambler. To become a winner, you must accept losing on a scale you would presently find unacceptable.'

Most punters mistakenly believe that the way to succeed at gambling is to pick as many winners as possible and this desire to win in the short-term adversely effects their chance of realising a decent profit over the course of a season. To succeed at this game you have to think in terms of odds and chances and understand that if you consistently back horses at odds lower than their true chance of winning you will lose, irrespective of the number of winners you achieve.

Punters back horses at unreasonably short odds because their egos are invested in their selections. Picking a winner is more important to them than the odds they obtain about it. Psychologically they would feel happier selecting five winners at 3-1 and ten losers, rather than one 25-1 winner and 14 losers even though the single winner would return a bigger profit. The five winners would provide a sense of security and a belief in their methods that the lone 25-1 winner would fail to achieve. Despite making a bigger profit, the 14 losers would leave them with a nagging doubt about their ability to pick enough winners in the long-term.

This need for the security of winners and an inability to deal with losers means punters are too quick to reject methods that do not select a good proportion of successful bets, irrespective of how profitable they might be over time. It also means that they look for the obvious contenders in a race, the ones with the best recent form that figure prominently in the betting market. Outsiders are anathema to them for they rarely boast such conspicuous credentials and they consider them to be inherently risky for they increase the likelihood of a dreaded 'losing run'. This conservative approach is endemic among punters and tipsters alike and it is one of the main reasons why so few are able to make a success of their betting.

During 2000 the *Racing Post* ran a 'National Press Challenge' that gave 13 newspaper tipsters a theoretical starting bank of £1,000 from which £1 was staked at SP on their selections. The result of the challenge demonstrates how conservative most tipsters are and how they simply ignore the concept of value in their quest to pick as many winners as possible. According to the *Racing Post*, issued on 4 November 2000, after 6,223 races the tipsters involved in the challenge had picked the favourite 47% of the time. Interestingly, despite the fact that their average winning strike rate was a respectable 26%, not one of them looked like showing a profit. The best's starting bank had been reduced from £1,000 to a pre-tax figure of £663 and the worst to a dismal £41! Betting shop punters would have lost an additional £560 in betting tax!

Although I have some sympathy for the tipsters because they faced an impossible task trying to analyse every race that was run, I do wonder sometimes why they get paid for making such mindless selections. Nevertheless, the example demonstrates that the majority of tipsters have a very similar perception of what constitutes a likely winner and, of course, the majority of punters follow their lead. Because so many people are backing the same horses their prices are artificially shortened and this makes it difficult to realise a profit even when achieving a decent winning strike rate.

THE IMPORTANCE OF GOOD-PRICED WINNERS

The result of another tipping contest the *Racing Post*'s 2000 Naps Competition is a good example of how adopting a different approach to the majority of punters can pay dividends. The competition, won by *Raceform*'s Mark Nelson, demonstrated how important big prices are in the long-term when it comes to maximising profits. He ran out a clear winner having selected several outstanding handicap winners such as Lady Boxer 50-1, Premier Baron 33-1, Chorus 20-1 and Muddy Water 16-1 to name but four, despite having one of the worst overall strike rates and suffering a run of 16 losers at one stage. On 4 November 2000 he led the field with a level stakes profit of +47 points, but with only 36 winners out of 198 bets (18%) he had the 13th worst strike rate out of the 60 competing tipsters! Tolerating a much higher percentage of losers than most punters would find acceptable, Mark Nelson's belief was that his strategy of backing horses at big prices in handicaps (the average odds of his winners was 5.8 to 1) would pay off over the course of the season. He was proven to be right.

The same naps competition produced some other interesting results. Keith McHugh, for instance, managed to select 85 winners at average odds of 15-8 and finished second overall with a level stakes profit of 43.5 points. His winning strike rate was an impressive 43%. Although a high proportion of his bets were placed on short-priced favourites in non-handicaps, his performance demonstrates that there is no right or wrong way to approach betting and that it is certainly possible to find value about horses returned at short odds.

The merit of McHugh's performance and his ability to identify value among short-priced favourites was highlighted by the results of Bob Watts and Alan Keyte. They managed to select 79 and 85 winners respectively and record strike rates of 41% and 45%, but remarkably were both nursing small level stakes losses on the last day of the competition. The average odds of their selections were 11-8 and 5-4 respectively and, although they found plenty of winners, they were not able to identify enough value bets to return a profit, unlike McHugh. The average longest losing run endured by the three of them was nine which demonstrates that even punters with very high overall strike rates are not immune from long losing sequences.

Although their methods would find favour with those punters who seek the security of a high winning strike rate, I find any approach that targets short-priced favourites unadventurous and rather sterile. I cannot get excited about a 5-4 winner that, after all, will cover little more than my next losing bet and any progress towards worthwhile profits is usually characterised by a rather unappealing steady plod. I believe that the only reason I was able to make a level stakes profit of 134 points during the 2000 Flat season was that I adopted an approach that concentrated on outsiders in handicaps. Like Mark Nelson, I was prepared to accept a high proportion of losers, but the big-priced winners I was able to find more than compensated for them. My progress towards worthwhile profits was certainly more of a rollercoaster than McHugh's, but ultimately the big-priced winners I found produced much larger profits.

OVERCOME THE FEAR OF LOSING

Of course it is not easy to identify an outsider with an obvious chance of winning because the bookmakers are seldom that generous! Outsiders rarely have everything in their favour and usually there are one or two question marks about their overall or recent form, which can be off-putting. Such doubts, however superficial, can trouble the conservative side of one's nature and it can be a struggle to see beyond them. It is one thing to be able to think differently to other punters and quite another to act differently! An unwillingness to place a speculative bet on a horse, even when you feel sure that the available odds more than compensate for the level of risk involved, will be the stumbling-block you are most likely to have difficulty overcoming.

Most of us have an in-built fear of losing and it can be hard to force yourself to bet when you know there is a good chance the horse will lose, irrespective of whether its winning chance is considerably better than its long odds suggest. This is a weakness that I am still struggling to overcome and I have missed out on some huge-priced winners as a result. Yes, I have also saved myself a lot of losers but I know that the winners I have missed would easily have compensated for them.

Take, for example, the case of Leaping Charlie who won at Ayr on 31 May 2001. This gelding had experienced training problems and only ran twice on turf during 2000. As a result he was well handicapped with an official rating 6lbs below his previous winning mark and, being a five-year-old, he was likely to have reached his physical peak. When he made his reappearance on turf at Ripon in 2001 he had not run for 83 days. Despite his possible lack of peak fitness he managed to finish fifth of 16, three lengths behind the winner in a five-furlong claimer. When I subsequently looked through the results section of the *Raceform Update* I realised that Leaping Charlie might well have produced a much-improved performance. On the prevailing soft ground his draw in stall nine would have been very difficult to overcome but he managed to 'win' the race that took place on the stands side by three lengths after the field had split into two groups. He easily beat two horses officially rated 20lbs above him and one horse that was rated 16lbs above him and, unless the three horses had all performed well below their best, Leaping Charlie must have improved.

When he reappeared 43 days later at Ayr, I was surprised to find that his official rating had remained unchanged and also that he was forecast to start at 25-1. However, although I thought long and hard about backing him I just could not bring myself to do it. I managed to convince myself that his Ripon run had been a freak result brought about by the very soft ground and that the horse was too unreliable. I had a nagging feeling that his forecast odds more than compensated for the doubts I had, but for whatever reason my conservative side that worries about having a loser kicked in and I declined to have a bet. Typically, I was left to rue that too defensive attitude – Leaping Charlie won nicely at the remarkably generous odds of 50-1! Although it is easy to say in hindsight, the huge odds easily compensated for the doubts I had and I certainly should have made that bet.

To highlight value outsiders, you need an approach that is not only based on sound and logical footings but is also different to the methods used by the majority of other people. When I studied the methods employed by most British tipsters and racing commentators, I found that, notable exceptions apart, the majority placed the most emphasis on the same factors such as good recent form, final time ratings, how horses are weighted in relation to each other and trainers and jockeys. I identified several shortcomings in their methods. Of course the fundamental weakness was that they were making very similar selections and they were accepting short odds as a result, but I also concluded that one of their basic beliefs was flawed.

THE FLAWED LOGIC OF TRADITIONAL HANDICAPPING

The accepted way to comprehend and quantify form in Britain is centred on the premise that it is possible to measure the ability of horses and that those differences in ability can be expressed in pounds. The idea is logical enough. If you have one horse that is faster than another you should be able to negate the difference between them by putting more weight on the back of the faster horse to slow it down. If it takes 20lbs of weight to bring their abilities together then the faster horse can justifiably be described as being 20lbs better than the slower horse. The logical extension of this theory is that if the faster horse only has to concede 15lbs to the slower horse it will beat it every time, but if it has to concede 25lbs it will lose.

This logic has led to the widely held belief that a horse's chance in a handicap race is determined by how much weight it is carrying in relation to its rivals. Although there is no doubt that weight has an influence on the outcome of races, its impact has been exaggerated and is not as important as the majority of punters consider it to be. If races took place under laboratory-style conditions I am sure that weight would have the effect it is supposed to, but in reality there are other equally important factors influencing a horse's performance and the theory is regularly undone by them.

Back in 1992, Nick Mordin suggested that punters should ignore weight and the method for producing speed figures that he espoused in *Betting For a Living* deliberately made no mention of it. Although his advice was largely ignored, of late there has been a noticeable reappraisal of the impact of weight and how it affects the accuracy of ratings that incorporate it. For example, *Raceform*'s 'Split Second' (Dave Bellingham) caused a stir among the paper's readers after announcing that his speed figures would no longer be weight-adjusted. However, I for one was in total agreement with the following justification he gave for his decision:

'The speed figures are not weight-adjusted so no further adjustments are necessary. This is by design, as it is not felt that any weight-adjustment formulae have been proven to be accurate – quite the opposite. Horses gaining or losing weight on their backs from one run to the next are not running faster or slower in relation, so other factors must be at work, such as the draw, ground, distance, fitness, etc.'

During its racing career a handicapper will inevitably produce poor performances, moderate performances and good performances and will attract very different ratings for them. The horse's actual ability can only be measured on those occasions when it produces its best and its other performances are meaningless as a guide to its capabilities other than to confirm dislikes and limitations. Although this is obvious enough, too many punters waste their time using past results and literal interpretations of who beat who and the distances and weights involved to determine how well handicapped horses are in relation to each other. These punters labour under the belief that if *exposed* horse **A** beat *exposed* horse **B** by three lengths in a five-furlong handicap it must be a 9lbs better handicapped horse (3 lengths x 3lbs = 9lbs). Horse **B** will only be able to reverse the placings in a future race if its official rating is 10lbs or more lower in relation to horse **A's**.

Those who believe this nonsense are effectively saying on the evidence of one race that the official ratings of the horses in question (ratings that are usually based on numerous past performances) were wildly inaccurate! Yes, *on the day* Horse **A** could be described as having beaten horse **B** by a margin theoretically equating to 9lbs, but that certainly does not mean that horse **A** is necessarily a 9lbs better handicapped horse. More often than not the difference between them on the day can be explained by the fact that Horse **A** was more favoured by the run of the race, the prevailing conditions and/or the track biases. Horse **A** can only be considered to have been 9lbs better handicapped than horse **B** if both horses were equally favoured by the conditions and either it was improving or horse **B** was deteriorating.

The use of collateral form as a tool with which to interpret handicaps simply compounds the error manifest in the above approach by adding another link to an already flimsy chain. Anybody advocating its use, or heard to utter the words 'on a line through...' when referring to handicap form deserves to be ridiculed! The theory suggests that if horse **A** has run against horse **B** and horse **B** has run against horse **C** then it is possible to determine the outcome of a contest between horse **A** and horse **C**. The belief is that by taking into account the distances between **A** and **B** and **B** and **C**, the weights each horse carried, and the weights **B** and **C** are set to carry, it is possible to determine which of the two horses is better handicapped. Again, under laboratory-type conditions the theory might just work but there are simply too many factors influencing how each horse performed, particularly from one race to another, for it to work in practice.

I have some sympathy for those that use this flawed approach to try to gauge the ability of two- and three-year-olds that have only made a few racecourse appearances because there is often precious little other evidence to draw on. However, there is no place for such guesswork in the analysis of all-aged handicaps.

I believe that the logical way to determine how well handicapped horses are in relation to each other is to decide how well treated each horse is in isolation, rather than drawing dubious conclusions from their past meetings or from meetings between them and a third horse. If I consider that horse **A** is capable of producing form that merits a rating of 90 but it is currently officially rated 87 and that horse **B** is capable of producing a rating of only 80 but is rated 84, I would argue that horse **A** is 7lbs better handicapped than horse **B** and my findings will not be influenced by how they have performed against each other or a third horse in the past.

THE IMPORTANCE OF BIASES

Another common failing in this country is that most punters ignore bias. Any analysis of handicap form that does not take racing's inherent biases into account is flawed for it is virtually impossible to make proper sense of form unless you are able to identify when it has been affected, either positively or negatively by them. This is hardly a new revelation as American racing authors have been writing about the importance of bias and other factors for years.

During the 1970s and 1980s a number of these writers transformed the study of form and managed to lend a subject that had been considered disreputable a basis in scholarship. William L. Quirin demonstrated that horses displaying early speed in a race were the most likely to win. Steve Davidowitz popularised the importance of track bias. Bonnie Ledbetter highlighted the importance of equine body language and physical appearance. Steve Roman created the dosage index and illustrated the relationship between a horse's breeding and its distance requirements. And Tom Ainslie demonstrated how factors such as class, age, sex and consistency can be used to identify the likely 'also-rans' in a race, and he encouraged punters to use a process of elimination to reduce a field to its logical contenders. The Americans understand that well-handicapped horses are well handicapped more as a consequence of bias and other factors than as a consequence of weight. Indeed this has become so ingrained in their approach to form study that they use the term 'handicapping' as a reference to the art of assessing a horse's chance in the light of all available information, rather than the art of assigning a horse a rating. Punters there are routinely referred to as 'handicappers'!

British writers such as Mordin and professional gambler Alan Potts have drawn on the works of the Americans for much of their inspiration, but despite their best efforts to educate the long-suffering punters in the UK, the majority remain uncomfortably tied to their systematic methods and unshakeable beliefs. I suspect that one of the reasons why the Americans have left us behind when it comes to understanding form is that they have had to strive to overcome the problems associated with their Tote-style pari-mutuels. Pool betting means that where a consensus approach exists among the betting public it becomes virtually impossible to realise a long-term profit because the pari-mutuels pay less as more money is bet on a horse and punters have no control over the final odds about their selection. It is irrelevant whether or not the accepted approach reflects an intelligent understanding of the winner-finding process because as soon as the majority of punters identify the same horse as being the likely winner any value evaporates and the method automatically becomes a losing one.

For British punters this problem is offset to a degree by the fact that they are able to take a price about their selections, but in America the only way to make a profit is to find a logical approach that is not widely used. The successful punters in the US have grasped that the art of showing a profit is not about developing ways to find more winners but is more to do with developing ways of being different.

THE NEED FOR A DIFFERENT APPROACH

In his book *Fast Tracks to Thoroughbred Profits* Mark Cramer took this idea a stage further. He introduced his concept of opposite logics to show that there is no right or wrong way to approach form study, and that in fact methods commonly held to be 'wrong' often present value opportunities simply because they are ignored by the majority of people. He argued that there is no permanent right way because the betting market will in time inevitably turn a winning way into a losing one. The Americans have come to recognise that this situation exists and that it calls for a fluidity of approach.

Punters need to be prepared to change tack each time the door closes on one avenue to profits and to understand that there are many logical approaches that can be adopted that are neither inherently right nor wrong. Some will fail because the selections are overbet while others will succeed only because they are overlaid. The bookmakers can close several doors at any one time but there will still be overlays for they cannot cover every angle without betting to grossly unfair over-rounds.

In *The Inside Track*, Alan Potts proved this very point when he detailed how the betting market had squeezed the profitability of the successful methods he had described in his earlier book *Against the Crowd*. Although Potts has successfully made a living from betting for many years he has been forced to adapt and develop his approach over that time in order to stay ahead of the game. Readers of his first book *Against the Crowd* who took his ideas on board and justifiably felt that they were sure to benefit from them, were probably surprised when reading *The Inside Track* only a few years later to find the following admission:

> 'The race epitomises the summer, a story of nearly, maybe, should have been – and biased stewards! But there was more to it than that. The methods I had used successfully for many years were no longer working. I had found my fair share of winners during the summer, but had passed on backing a good many of them because the price was too short. Every time I found a value bet that paid off, I either messed up the staking, or gave back the profits within days.'

With the benefit of hindsight perhaps a more pertinent title for his first book would have been *Too Similar to the Crowd!*

For whatever reason the market was no longer allowing Potts to obtain sufficient value about his selections to realise a profit and he was forced to accept the inevitable that he needed to develop a new approach. He had no clear idea of what that new approach might be and it was not until after he had read a number of books by some of the US authors that he found a way forward. What he wrote about this is informative:

> 'It took a while for the penny to drop, and then I realised that the most signifi-cant thing about all these American punters was not what they wrote about, but what they never mentioned. They seemed to have no interest in form in the sense that it is understood in this country. When writing about an individual horse, they rarely mentioned the horses it had run against. They simply weren't interested in who had beaten it, or whom it had beaten, let alone the distances or weight involved. Although different writers placed the greatest emphasis on different factors, the principal concerns of all of them were the same – speed figures, pace and track bias ... When analysing future races, they were searching for clues as

15

to the shape of the race. Who would lead? How fast would they go? Where is the fastest strip on the track? And is the track favouring front-runners, or fast finishers?'

Having taken the American methodology on board, Potts centred his new approach on speed figures, pace and draw bias. But he also learned to profit from predicting how races were likely to unfold and by anticipating where horses would be positioned at key stages – an art that most punters here had little or no understanding of. Because his new approach was totally different to those adopted by other punters in this country it proved to be profitable and Potts felt that his betting had progressed to a new level. His experiences endorse Mark Cramer's argument that there is no permanently 'right way' and that to enjoy continued success you have to be prepared to adapt and evolve your methods to ensure that they remain different to those employed by other punters.

Although my betting also improved markedly after I adopted the American style approach explained in this book, I am aware that it is becoming harder to maintain the edge it has given me. It is noticeable that tipsters and racing journalists are becoming ever more conscious of bias and Melvyn Collier (former Pricewise in the *Racing Post*) in particular, has done a lot to educate punters in this regard. I have often found that Collier and his successors have put up the horse that I want to back and irritatingly its price is invariably slashed before I have a chance to place a bet.

The better 'telephone tipping' lines also cause a similar market reaction when they put a horse up and the high level of competition for the available value can be frustrating at times. It means that I have had to work harder and delve deeper, but I accept that I need to keep searching for other angles and sources of information that are not commonly employed if I want to maintain an edge. If your aim is to become a more successful bettor you too will need to concentrate your efforts on finding ways to be different that have a basis in logic, instead of wasting your time trying to develop ways to pick more short-priced winners.

CHAPTER TWO

WHAT IS THE HORSE'S STYLE OF RUNNING?

It is easy to be taken in by a held-up horse that appeared unlucky not to win when finishing late and seemingly fast on its last outing. It is also easy to believe that had the jockey begun his effort a little earlier, or had the horse enjoyed a clearer run, then it would have won. Such horses routinely capture the betting public's imagination and they are invariably well supported next time they run. Most commentators and racing journalists encourage this misplaced confidence by extolling the virtues of any runner that appears to finish 'with a wet sail' and their notebooks are crammed with seemingly unlucky losers that 'should not be missed next time'!

The truth, however, is that most of these horses flatter only to deceive and there is a simple explanation for this. At most racetracks it is a positive disadvantage to be held-up and horses that are raced in this way face the same problems nearly every time they run. They are at the mercy of the runners that set the early pace because their chance is dependent to a large degree on there being a strong early gallop. The jockey's judgement of pace and his ability to time his run are especially tested and as always horses coming from behind need luck when it comes to obtaining a clear run. Whilst everything needs to fall into place for held-up horses to win, those that race prominently face fewer difficulties and the statistics show that they have a superior winning record as a result. There is no doubt that the position of a horse in the early stages of a race has a significant bearing on its chance and the following table shows that at most British racetracks horses that hold a prominent position have a definite advantage that should not be underestimated.

DISTANCE	MID-DIVISION AND BEHIND	CHASED LEADERS	LED AND PROMINENT
5F & 6F	419 WINS (33%) **0.67**	313 WINS (25%) **1.04**	524 WINS (42%) **1.61**
7F , 8F, 9F	570 WINS (40%) **0.81**	354 WINS (25%) **1.05**	484 WINS (35%) **1.32**
10F+	852 WINS (49%) **0.98**	382 WINS (22%) **0.92**	510 WINS (29%) **1.12**
TOTAL	1841 WINS (42%) **0.84**	1049 WINS (24%) **0.99**	1518 WINS (34%) **1.32**

The table incorporates the results of those handicaps run during the last four seasons that had at least eight contestants. The runners were divided into three groups and each group is made up of horses that were described as having raced in a particular way. The figures in bold compare the number of winners each group had to the number of winners they should have had. Horses that are held back in mid-division and behind in the early stages of a race account for 50% of the runners on average and should therefore account for 50% of the winners. Horses that race prominently account for 26% of the runners and those that chase the leaders make up the other 24%. In theory each group should record a figure of **1.0** because their percentage of winners should be the same as their percentage of runners and any variant shows that a bias exists. A figure of **2.0** means that the group wins twice as often as it should and a figure of **0.5** means that it wins half as often as it should and so on.

What group each horse was placed in depended on the comment it attracted from the race readers and the qualifying comments for the three groups were as follows:

Led and Prominent: led, prominent, speed, close up, pressed leader, pressed leaders, chased winner, chased leader, tracked leader, tracked winner.

Chased Leaders: chased leaders, tracked leaders, in touch.

Mid-Division and Behind: mid-division, behind, rear, never dangerous, 'held up, headway...'

Note that the comment 'held up' on its own does not indicate a position towards the rear of the field. It is possible to be 'held up in touch' or 'held up behind leaders' which belong to the Chased Leaders category. It is the comment after 'held up' that describes the horse's position in the early stages of a race.

The statistics prove that horses racing prominently in the early stages of a race are the most likely to win and although the gap narrows as the distances get longer, in the majority of cases the front is the place to be. Horses that show the speed to race prominently for the first few furlongs of a race often put a gap between themselves and the rest that proves too difficult to close. In most instances the leaders do not tire quickly enough and those that are held up need to accelerate to close on them.

However, there are not many handicappers that can quicken noticeably in the final stages of a race and although it frequently appears that horses are accelerating from the rear it is more often than not an illusion. The gap appears to close fast only because the leaders are unable to maintain their early speed to the end of the race and slow markedly towards the finish. The held-up horses seem to be accelerating but they are usually simply running on at the same pace whilst the leaders are weakening.

Those at the front are less likely to encounter trouble in running than those towards the back. The ones at the rear can experience difficulty obtaining a clear run, and it is not uncommon for the latter to be hampered either by weakening horses dropping back through the field, or by other held-up horses that are competing for the same gaps. The prominent horses also have the advantage of being able to race on the best ground throughout a race and they can save valuable ground on the turns by taking the shortest route home next to the rails.

Although it is an advantage to race up with the pace in races up to nine furlongs at the majority of tracks, there are two notable exceptions to the rule and they are Bath and Newbury. At Bath, horses that race prominently in sprint races have a pace figure of **0.8** and are at a disadvantage, particularly in large fields. In his book *The Inside Track* Alan Potts offered the following explanation: 'Mark Holder pointed out that front runners rarely seemed to win sprints at Bath, despite the apparent advantage they should have from racing next to the bend three furlongs out, and the elbow just before the furlong marker. I watched some films and concluded that front runners were losing momentum at the elbow by changing their legs. Having used their speed to be in front at that point, they couldn't pick up again during the final furlong. A horse challenging on the outside wouldn't notice the elbow at all and wouldn't check its stride at any stage.'

I think Potts' assessment is the right one and it also helps to explain why the horses drawn wide in stalls 16 to 20 have the best draw figure of **1.5**. Their wide early position allows them to approach the tight bends from a less acute angle than those drawn nearer to the inside rail and they do not have to check their stride. Furthermore, the wide horses are more likely to be held up than those drawn low because their riders want to avoid losing too much ground round the turns and a relationship exists between the draw and pace biases. It may pay to concentrate on horses drawn wide that are usually held up for a late run when analysing big-field sprint races at Bath!

In general, the advantage held by the prominent horses is less significant in races of ten furlongs or more and at many of the tracks it is preferable to be held up in the early stages of these contests. As a rule the longer the distance the harder it becomes to win from the front. I am not sure why this should be but it appears to be an advantage to conserve energy in the initial part of long-distance events and horses that go off in front invariably tire badly in the closing stages unless they have been able to dictate a modest pace. Whatever the reasons the pace charts in this chapter will help you to identify where it is best to race prominently and where it is best to be held up for a late challenge. This knowledge will subtly shift the odds of success in your favour and will help you to avoid silly bets on horses whose chances of winning are virtually precluded by their running style.

WHAT TACTICS WILL THE HORSE EMPLOY?

Determining the position a horse will hold in a race is definitely more of an art than a science but it is possible to get it right most of the time. Although you cannot hope to anticipate the sudden changes in tactics that are at the whim of connections, in most cases a horse's last three races are a good guide to how it will run. If a horse has been prominent in the early stages of its last three runs it is likely to be prominent again.

There are, however, a number of factors that can influence the tactics that connections decide to employ. For example, the characteristics of the track and the stall a horse has been allocated often determine the effect a horse's early position in a race has on its chance of winning; connections may take these factors into account before deciding on tactics. At Chester, for example, horses that race prominently have a big advantage over sprint distances (pace figure **2.6**) and those that are held up in rear have little chance (**0.4**). However, runners drawn out wide seldom attempt to race prominently even if they normally blaze a trail in their races. If they stay out wide on a turning track such as Chester, they have to travel many lengths further than the runners on the inside and they invariably struggle to overtake them as a result. Because of this they are usually restrained and moved over towards the inside by their riders who take a gamble on obtaining a clear run as the race unfolds. For this reason the pace figures exaggerate the importance of racing prominently at Chester because they are skewed by the fact that most badly-drawn horses are forced to race towards the back of the field, while a higher proportion of well-drawn horses race prominently. This is also true at a number of other tracks.

In the United States it is comparatively easy to predict which horses will race prominently because punters there not only have access to sectional times, but races are also divided into 'calls' and their form summaries record every runner's position and distance behind the leader at each call. Although this information would obviously simplify the process of predicting the early pace for punters in Britain, I will not join the clamour for the introduction of sectional timing at all of our tracks. If this information was widely available it would be harder for people like me to gain an edge by improvising and obtaining it by other means. Remember, becoming a more successful punter is not about finding a greater number of winners but is about finding ways of being different!

THE IMPORTANCE OF SPEED POINTS

It was William Quirin, Professor of Mathematics at Adelphi University, who, having realised the importance of early pace, first developed and successfully employed a method for assigning speed points to horses to predict which runners would vie for the early lead. His research had shown that horses in the first three at the first 'call' won five out of every nine races, returning a profit equivalent to 28 pence for each pound invested. He also found that a horse with a clear lead (one length or more) at the first call won three times more often than it should and returned a profit of 80 pence on each pound invested!

I confess that when I first read this I was astonished. I suspected that the extraordinary success of the front runners must have been peculiar to the US's dirt tracks. I know that dirt favours front runners because the held-up horses find it hard to accelerate on the loose surface; I suspected that the leaders were also favoured by the tight nature of many of the courses. However, having conducted my own research I was surprised to discover that front runners were also strongly favoured on Britain's turf courses and that there was only a small difference between the bias described by Quirin and that indicated by my findings. The table below is based on data drawn from four seasons and only includes the results of handicap races that had eight or more runners.

HORSES THAT TAKE THE EARLY LEAD					
DISTANCE	NUMBER OF RACES	AVERAGE NUMBER OF RUNNERS PER RACE	EXPECTED NUMBER OF LEADERS TO WIN	ACTUAL NUMBER OF LEADERS THAT WIN	WIN RATIO
5F & 6F	1,256	15.38	81.66	208	2.55
7F & 8F	1,221	15.34	79.6	215	2.7
9F+	1,772	13.28	133.4	209	1.57
TOTALS	4,249		294.6	632	2.14

Quirin found that horses with a clear early lead won three times more often than expected. My figures show that in this country horses with any sort of lead win over twice as often as they should and that over the optimum trips of seven and eight furlongs they have a remarkable win ratio of **2.7**. A horse that leads a race in the initial stages has a significant advantage and it is certainly worthwhile trying to predict which one will do so. This is one of the most powerful biases and by way of a comparison there are only a handful of draw positions that confer a similar advantage.

Quirin's speed point method involved awarding horses points based on both their position and their distance behind the leader at the first 'call' and proved to be an accurate predictor of those runners that contest the early pace. Our different form summaries mean that it is not possible to tell how far behind the leader each horse was in the early stages of their previous races. However, it is possible to get a good idea of their position by interpreting the race comments and speed points can be allocated accordingly. I have adapted Quirin's method to suit our form summaries and I use the first comment a horse is given for each of its last three races. In other words if the description was **'held up rear, pushed along to lead halfway, weakened final furlong'** the relevant comment is 'rear' and if the description was **'prominent, effort to lead three out, ridden clear final furlong'** the relevant comment is 'prominent'. I then award speed points to each horse as follows:

Four Points: made all, led

Two Points: speed, prominent, close up, pressed leader, pressed winner, chased winner, chased leader, tracked leader, tracked winner.

The horse with the most cumulative points is the one likely to lead. Although this basic method works well enough, because of the importance of being able to predict the early leader it is worth devoting a little extra time to improve its accuracy by taking into account other factors. Perhaps the most obvious of these is the number of runners in a qualifying race. Logically it is easier to race prominently in small fields than it is in large ones and in order to factor this into the equation I deduct one point if there were eight or fewer runners and add one point if there were 25 or more runners. It is a good idea to take split fields into account here and to check the number of runners in each split.

The distance of the qualifying race also needs to be considered. If a horse has been racing over shorter trips it may have been unable to race as prominently as usual because it lacked the speed to keep up over the shorter distance. While if it has been racing over longer trips it will have found it easier to take an early lead. As I have already mentioned the draw can also have an impact. Horses racing on slower ground or drawn wide on a turning track will struggle to race prominently and you need to make allowances for this. If you spot that a horse's chance of racing prominently was negatively affected by these factors it is a good idea to ignore that particular performance. Indeed, Quirin recommended awarding a horse a 'bye' in these circumstances and to allocate it points from its next most recent race instead. To do this you will normally need access to the results 'pull outs' from *Raceform Update* because the *Racing Post* often only provides the form for a horse's last three runs.

Once I have awarded points to all the runners I draw a diagram similar to the one below to show how the pace in the race is spread across the field. Note that in the example the highest stall number is situated on the left to reflect the actual layout of the starting stalls when you view them from the front.

STALL	22	21	20	19	18	17	16	15	14	13	12	11	10	9	8	7	6	5	4	3	2	1
PACE FIGURE	6	0	0	0	0	2	0	0	0	0	NR	0	NR	1	6	4	0	0	0	NR	0	4
TOTAL			>8<											>15<								

This example is taken from the five-furlong handicap run at York on 16 June 2000 (see page 65 for more details [The Theory In Practice]. I backed Storyteller each-way at 20-1 chiefly because the horse was positioned in stall 2. The draw bias at York had been favouring the low to middle numbers for some time and after I produced the above figures I felt sure that with nearly twice as much pace on that side of the track the low numbers would dominate the race. In the event Storyteller finished third and the first seven home were drawn 5, 4, 2, 8, 22, 9, 6. The only horse drawn high to trouble the low numbers was Further Outlook who raced prominently throughout from stall 22, as the chart suggested he would. The horses that raced prominently or chased the leaders in the race were drawn in stalls 1, 2, 5, 7, 8, 15, 16, 19, 21, 22 and among them were four of the five horses awarded more than one pace point.

In order to estimate the chance of the horse with the most speed points taking the lead and the advantage it might hold, William Quirin recommended calculating its 'speed point percentage'. Suppose the speed points in a ten-runner race are 8-5-0-0-2-3-4-1-0-2 then the total number of points is 25. To calculate the percentage you simply divide the cumulative figure of the horse with the most speed points into the overall total, which in this example would be 8 divided by 25 (32%). American studies have shown that horses with 'speed point percentages' of 30% or more are likely to take the lead and they have an increased chance of winning.

A good example of how this theory can work in practice was at Haydock on 7 June 2001. Of the eight runners in the race, six were confirmed held-up types and they attracted no pace points. However, the lightly-raced four-year-old colt Takamaka Bay had led in the early stages of all three of his races to date and was clearly an out-and-out front runner. He attracted nine pace points rather than twelve because none of his previous races had had more than eight runners. The only other horse that had raced prominently in any of its last three races was Faraway Look who was awarded four pace points. Takamaka Bay's speed point percentage was thus 69% (nine divided by 13). This suggested that he would enjoy an uncontested lead and it was very likely that he would be allowed to dictate the pace and keep enough in reserve to run on in the final stages. The held-up types were likely to have to accelerate in the final few furlongs to close on him – something that was likely to prove beyond them.

Despite the clear chance the pace figures indicated, Takamaka Bay was fourth in the betting forecast at 6-1. In the event he made all, holding on well from Faraway Bay, who was the only serious challenger and who was returned at 11-2.

THE SHAPE OF THE RACE

Pace figures can also be used to determine the 'shape' of a race and to predict how it will develop. They show how many front runners there are and where they are drawn. This information can be used to predict how strong the pace is likely to be and whether it is concentrated in a particular area of the track. In races run on straight courses it is important to know whether the pace is likely to be stronger on one side of the track or the other as it is usually an advantage to be drawn on the side where the pace is strongest. I say usually because it is an irrelevant consideration if there is a significant draw bias at the course. The well-drawn horses will normally dominate irrespective of where the pace lies. On those occasions when the position of the front runners coincides with the bias, the winner invariably comes from that part of the track.

If there are two or more confirmed front runners in a race the pace will normally be strong and the leaders are likely to tire quickly in the closing stages, particularly in races of nine furlongs or more. Whether this plays into the hands of the held-up horses depends on the track. If the course strongly favours this group anyway then the winner is almost certain to come from it, but if the course favours the prominent runners it is often a horse that chases or tracks the leaders that benefits most from the strong pace. Any horse that is awarded eight or more pace points will usually vie for the early lead. If you wish to get a rough idea of the position other horses are likely to take during the race then place the 25% with the highest pace points in the Led and Prominent group, the next 25% in the Chased Leaders group and the others in the Mid-division and Behind group. If there are no confirmed front runners in the race the early pace will probably be modest and if so, the advantage will lie with the horses that race prominently. If the track naturally favours front runners the winner will invariably come from the prominent group.

It is important to consider how a horse's style of running will affect any theoretical draw advantage it might hold. On many occasions well-drawn horses are beaten by the way they are ridden. When a well drawn horse is held up towards the rear the theoretical advantage it has often turns into a positive disadvantage, particularly in big fields and when there are bends to negotiate. The poorly-drawn runners invariably tack across to the favoured side and a horse that is held up inevitably finds itself behind a wall of runners and often gets shuffled further back by scrimmaging. In the final stages of the race it is likely to find its preferred passage blocked and may be forced to switch to the outside to make its run on the unfavoured part of the track!

Held-up horses can also be disadvantaged by being drawn widest of all for they may have to forfeit several lengths in the early stages of a race whilst moving over to find cover behind the main group of horses. Ideally this type of horse would have a middle draw on a straight track that does not confer much of a draw advantage.

CHAPTER THREE

THE DRAW AND HOW TO PRODUCE DRAW FIGURES

Before the running of the Group Two Tripleprint Temple Stakes over five furlongs on heavy ground at Sandown on 29 May 2000, most punters would have found it difficult to make much of a case for the chance of Perryston View. The eight year-old was an exposed handicapper who had been well beaten when stepped up to Group Three company earlier in the season. Also he was up against Sampower Star who was a proven Group Three performer rated 114, Imperial Beauty rated 113 and Rambling Bear rated 112. Although Perryston View was rated 107 following a convincing handicap win on his first run of the season, the highest rating he had previously won off was 98 and at his age he was unlikely to be improving, despite having recently moved to a new trainer. On the face of it his form was simply not good enough, but Perryston View managed to trounce the field, making all to win by five lengths, beating Imperial Beauty and Sampower Star by 11 lengths and 14 lengths respectively. Odds of 16-1 had been available that morning!

Without an understanding of the effect of the draw at Sandown the result would have been hard to forecast. However, both Pricewise and Spotlight of the *Racing Post* selected the horse and proved that it was possible to predict the outcome. They were aware that a high draw is vital on the straight course, particularly when the ground is heavy, and because Perryston View had the best draw in stall ten they were wisely prepared to ignore the fact that on paper he appeared to hold little chance at the weights. They identified that the first and second favourites Sampower Star and Imperial Beauty had little chance from stalls 3 and 1 and that the 16-1 about Perryston View was simply too big a price. There were ten runners in the race and the first three home were drawn 10, 8 and 9.

According to handicap theory Perryston View's performance was 36lbs better than that of Imperial Beauty and 42lbs better than that of Sampower Star. Although the margin of victory was exaggerated by the heavy ground, the effect of the draw on the outcome of the race was plain to see. The result demonstrates that under certain circumstances the only thing that really matters is the stall that each horse is allocated before it runs.

The effect the draw had on the race was highlighted by subsequent events. Perryston View's next run was in the Group Two King's Stand Stakes at Ascot where he again met Imperial Beauty on the same weight terms. On this occasion Imperial Beauty had a better draw and she turned the tables in convincing fashion, finishing fourth of 23 runners, seven lengths ahead of her Sandown conqueror who trailed in a disappointing 19th. Perryston View then had a lengthy break. On his second run after returning to the track he met Sampower Star in a Group One race at Haydock. They were drawn next to each other and despite re-opposing on the same weight terms Sampower Star beat Perryston View by six lengths! In reality Perryston View was not genuinely of Group Two class for he had been flattered by his win at Sandown, and his lofty revised rating of 116 was not merited. The subsequent turning over of the form no doubt left many punters scratching their heads, but with an understanding of the power of the draw it was entirely predictable.

Although this example is an extreme one it nevertheless provides a useful reminder of the impact that bias can have on a race. The draw bias was the arbiter of who won and who lost the race at Sandown and any analysis undertaken of the horses' ratings, of weight carried and how they had performed against each other in the past proved to be completely irrelevant!

At every Flat racecourse in the country, at some time or other, certain draw positions are favoured and others are disadvantaged. It is not always possible to predict before a race where the bias will lie but you can get it right most of the time if you equip yourself with the right information. Although the draw figures in this chapter should prove invaluable to you they are not the Holy Grail. They are a reliable guide but things can alter quite quickly for all sorts of reasons and it is important to remain alert to developments and to keep your statistics up to date. For example, past races were no guide to the strong bias that appeared dramatically and quite unexpectedly at Newmarket's July course on 11 July 2000, following the decision taken by the officials there to move the stands rail to reveal a fresh strip of ground. For whatever reason the new strip had not been affected by the recent rain to the same extent as the rest of the course, hence it was considerably firmer. The stalls were placed on the far side that day and their position handed a big advantage to the horses drawn towards the stands side. The winners on the straight course were drawn **8** (11 ran), **15** (18 ran), **11** (11 ran), **7** (8 ran), **12** (14 ran) and **11** (11 ran) and once again the only thing that really mattered was the stall each horse had been allotted.

The following day an embarrassed clerk of the course moved the stalls to the stands rail in an attempt to reduce the bias. Although it remained very much in evidence, interestingly the results proved hard to anticipate with three horses managing to win from low draws! Their jockeys had learned the lesson of the previous day and bounced their mounts quickly out of the stalls before tacking across to the faster ground. Making all along the stands rail, they ensured in the process that any challenger would be forced to go wide onto the slower ground to get past them. Their race-winning manoeuvres illustrate the relationship that does exist between early pace and draw bias.

Horses can overcome a poor draw if they have sufficient early speed to go clear of their rivals and then move across after the first one hundred yards or so to the faster ground. Although this manoeuvre is hard to execute on turning tracks such as Chester, where horses forfeit too much ground running wide round the bend in the initial stages, on straight courses it is comparatively easy to achieve if the horse is blessed with early speed. It is advisable to check for badly drawn front runners and to decide whether they are likely to be able to improve their position. The number of other front runners and whether they are drawn between the horse in question and the faster ground will have a bearing on this. However, if you think that a front runner will be able to go clear of the field in the early stages its chance should not be dismissed on account of its poor draw.

HOW TO PRODUCE DRAW STATISTICS

If you are serious about your betting you should go to the trouble of producing your own draw statistics. Although the tables in this book provide you with an up-to-date and comprehensive guide to the biases at each course, bear in mind that they can change quickly and that some of the statistics in this book will soon be obsolete. Factors such as the increased and selective use of watering, the installation of new drainage systems or the movement of the running rails can dramatically alter the bias, and it is easy to be caught out unless you regularly update your records.

Disturbingly, some clerks of the course are attempting to negate draw bias by watering certain parts of their tracks more heavily than others. Whilst a bias-free contest might be in the interests of the horses' owners, I doubt whether I am the only bettor who finds this trend irritating, particularly as there is little or no publicity about these artificial alterations. This tinkering more often than not simply causes the bias to shift to another part of the track rather than eliminating it! Several seasons ago the low-numbered stalls at Ripon's sprint course were hugely favoured but this advantage has now all but disappeared since the increased use of watering at the course. At Redcar watering has not only done away with the traditional advantage held by the high numbers on the straight course, but has made a high draw a positive disadvantage.

On 7 July 2000, I backed That Man Again in a race over Sandown's sprint course primarily because he was drawn 14 out of 14. He performed poorly and I was peeved to read after the race an admission by the clerk of the course that he had sought to reduce the draw bias by adopting a different watering policy. He had been encouraged by the more even spread, draw wise, of the two sprints! Strangely enough I could not recall coming across an article advertising this very significant policy change *prior* to the race, but this came as no surprise given the poor standard of information that punters have to put up with! I suppose such attempts to artificially alter the bias do have one benefit – the more changeable the biases become the more rewarding good, up-to-date statistics will be.

The draw statistics in this book (see page 83) are taken from the results of handicap races only. It is not a good idea to use the results of other races because they regularly include horses that are much better than their rivals. Without the levelling effect of weight they could win from virtually any draw in most cases, causing the worth of the statistics to be devalued. A lot of draw statistics are also devalued because they simply record each stall's wins to runners percentages and they fail to take into account how many times each stall *should* win. This is a significant omission.

Consider for example sprint races at Ripon, which are restricted to a maximum of 23 runners. Stall one is represented in every sprint race run at Ripon unless it houses a non-runner and its theoretical chance of winning varies from race to race depending on the size of the field. In a ten-runner race it has a 10% chance of winning, in a 16-runner race it has a 6.25% chance of winning and in a 20-runner race it has a 5% chance and so on. Stall 23 on the other hand is only filled when there is a maximum field of 23 and its best theoretical chance of winning a race is 4.3%. Therefore, when drawing the statistics from fields of eight runners or more, stalls one to eight should in theory house the highest and the same number of winners, whereas stall nine to 23 should produce progressively fewer winners. This has to be taken into account otherwise the high numbers will appear to do less well than they do in reality.

COMPILING THE DATA

The first step is to compile the data. I use the results of handicaps that had eight runners or more during the last five years. Results from earlier seasons are suspect because the advantage can change over time. If the draw bias *has* clearly altered during the last five seasons it is sensible to only use the figures from races run *after* the bias changed, even if this means there is limited evidence to draw on. When compiling a record of past results you have to make a note of where the stalls were positioned (i.e. high, centre or low), the state of the going, the winning stall number and the number of runners. Once the data has been gathered the next step is to write down how many winners and how many runners each stall housed and to list them in a format similar to the one below.

STALL	WINS	RUNNERS
1	6	52
2	3	52
3	5	52
etc.	etc.	etc.

The figures have to be entered differently depending on what side of the course the stalls were positioned (i.e. HIGH or LOW). If the stalls were LOW (i.e. the number one stall was positioned against one of the running rails) the lowest numbered stall should be entered as stall one and the second lowest numbered stall as stall two etc. However, if the stalls were HIGH (i.e. the highest numbered stall was positioned against one of the running rails) the figures need to be inverted and the highest numbered stall should be entered as stall one and the second highest numbered stall as stall two and so on. If you do not invert the figures in this way you may not be able to identify the bias. To show you what I mean take a look at the following results from Sandown's sprint course. In this example the stalls were positioned HIGH but to illustrate the point stall one has nevertheless erroneously been entered as stall one.

STALL	WINS	RUNS	PERCENTAGE
1	0	39	0%
2	4	39	10%
3	1	39	3%
4	2	39	5%
5	4	39	10%
6	1	39	3%
7	3	39	8%
8	2	39	5%
9	4	37	11%
10	5	33	15%
11	2	30	7%
12	4	21	19%
13	3	15	20%
14	3	9	33%
15	0	4	0%
16	0	2	0%
17	0	2	0%
18	1	1	100%

Although the figures suggest that the middle to high numbers do best they are rather inconclusive. With the exception of stall one, all the stalls appear to have a fair chance of winning, including stalls 15 to 17 (in view of the limited number of runners they housed it would be wrong to dismiss their chance as the stalls on either side scored well). There does not appear to be any significant bias. However, the figures mask the fact that horses racing against the far rail (HIGH) enjoy a significant advantage and those drawn out towards the middle of the track have virtually no chance of winning! The only way to obtain the true picture is to invert the figures and enter the highest numbered stall (the one placed against the favoured rail) as stall 1 and the next highest as stall 2 and so on. Have a look at the following table that shows the above results from Sandown after they have been inverted:

DRAW	WINS	RUNS	PERCENTAGE	
1	7	39	18%	
2	10	39	26%	18%
3	4	39	10%	
4	1	39	3%	
5	5	39	13%	6%
6	1	39	3%	
7	1	39	3%	
8	5	39	13%	5%
9	0	37	0%	
10	2	33	6%	
11	1	31	3%	5%
12	1	23	4%	
13	1	16	6%	
14	0	11	0%	2%
15	0	5	0%	
16	0	3	0%	
17	0	1	0%	0%
18	0	1	0%	

The inverted figures reveal that the highest numbered stalls actually enjoy a big advantage. Stalls 1 to 3 have an average wins to runs record of 18%, which is nearly three times the strike rate of the next three highest stalls. Those drawn out towards the middle of the track, ten or more places away from the far rail, have virtually no chance and might as well stay at home!

Once you have decided whether to invert the figures or not and you have worked out how many runners and how many winners each stall housed, the next step is to calculate how many winners each stall *should* have housed in theory. To do this, start with the stall with the least number of runners and work upwards. If stall 24 had only two runners the calculation is 2 divided by 24 = 0.083. If stall 23 had nine runners the calculation is 7 divided by 23 = 0.304. Stall 23's theoretical chance of housing a winner is thus 0.304 + 0.083 = 0.387 for it housed two runners with a 0.041 chance and seven runners with a 0.043 chance. If stall 22 had 13 runners the calculation is 4 divided by 22 (13 minus the 9 runners already accounted for) = 0.181. Stall 22's theoretical chance of housing a winner is 0.181 + 0.387 = 0.568 and so on. The table below shows the process in full.

The draw figure in the right hand column is calculated by dividing the theoretical accumulated winning chance of a stall into the number of winners it housed. In this example stall 2 housed 13 winners and the theoretical number of winners it should have had was 4.88 so the calculation is 13 divided by 4.88, which gives a draw figure of 2.66. If no bias exists each stall should theoretically have a draw figure of 1.0, so stall 2 in this example has housed a winner over two and a half times more often than it should have.

STALL	NUMBER OF RUNNERS	WINNING CHANCE		ACCUMULATED WINNING CHANCE	WINNERS	DRAW FIGURE
1	70			4.88	4	0.82
2	70	–		4.88	13	2.66
3	70	–		4.88	3	0.61
4	70	–		4.88	2	0.41
5	70	–		4.88	5	1.02
6	70	–		4.88	6	1.23
7	70	–		4.88	3	0.61
8	70	0.38	(3 x 0.125)	4.88	5	1.02
9	67	0.33	(3 x 0.11)	4.51	0	0.00
10	64	0.50	(5 x 0.10)	4.18	1	0.24
11	59	0.82	(9 x 0.09)	3.68	2	0.54
12	50	0.08	(1 x 0.083)	2.86	4	1.39
13	49	0.23	(3 x 0.077)	2.78	3	1.08
14	46	0.21	(3 x 0.071)	2.55	1	0.39
15	43	0.27	(4 x 0.067)	2.34	1	0.43
16	39	0.56	(9 x 0.062)	2.07	1	0.48
17	30	0.29	(4 x 0.058)	1.51	3	1.99
18	26	0.22	(4 x 0.055)	1.22	0	0.00
19	22	0.10	(2 x 0.053)	1.00	4	4.00
20	20	0.15	(3 x 0.05)	0.90	0	0.00
21	17	0.19	(4 x 0.048)	0.75	4	5.33
22	13	0.18	(4 x 0.045)	0.56	2	3.57
23	9	0.30	(7 x 0.043)	0.38	0	0.00
24	2	0.08	(2 x 0.04)	0.08	1	12.5

The next step is to produce average draw figures because some of the individual ones should not be taken at face value. For example, although stalls 20 and 23 housed no winners they are sandwiched between stalls that boast high draw figures and their poor record can be attributed to the limited number of runners they housed. In time they are sure to have their share of winners. The draw figure of 12.5 awarded to stall 24 should not be taken at face value either because it has been distorted by the fact that it housed one winner from only two runners and it is has no chance of maintaining such a high strike rate in the long-term.

To obtain a fairer impression it is necessary to divide the stalls into groups and calculate the average of each group's figures. The average can then be viewed alongside the individual figure for each stall and it often helps to make sense of what is sometimes a jumbled-looking picture. The way to do this is to add up the accumulated chance of the stalls in each group and divide the sum into the group's total number of winners. I vary the size of the groups depending on the course because the maximum number of runners at each track varies markedly and the greater the maximum field size the bigger the groups need to be. The table below shows the above draw figures after they have been averaged.

STALLS	WINS	ACCUMULATED CHANCE	AVERAGE FIGURE
1 – 4	22	19.52	1.22
5 – 8	19	19.52	0.97
9 –12	7	15.23	0.45
13 – 16	6	9.74	0.61
17 – 20	7	4.63	1.51
21 – 24	7	1.77	3.95

The average figures provide a much clearer picture and they show that the most favoured stalls in this example are 21 to 24, which win nearly four times more often than they should. Stalls 1 to 4 and 17 to 20 are positive draws as well, but 9 to 16 are coffin draws; horses housed in them are likely to perform poorly unless they are able to quickly improve their position by taking an early lead and tacking across to the faster ground.

Non-runners can skew the figures so they need to be considered. Their effect is minimal when the stalls are 'Low' but whenever the stalls are 'High' and the figures are consequently inverted, they can cause the highest few numbers to be unfairly favoured unless an adjustment is made. If a race has 16 runners you would normally assume that the highest stall number in the race was 16. However, if there are non-runners this is not the case. If there are three non-runners the highest stall number is potentially 19 and as a result the highest stall in the race which should be entered as stall 1 can *appear* to be either stall 19, 18, 17, or 16 unless you study the stall numbers in the race closely. It is easy to fall into the trap of entering any of the above four stalls as stall 1 when you are quickly skimming through past results extracting the data. Obviously you need to ascertain what the highest-numbered stall was and enter that as stall 1.

WAYS TO USE THE DRAW FIGURES

Without a doubt the most useful thing about draw figures is that they offer a way to eliminate runners from further consideration when you are analysing a race. I prefer to concentrate on those handicaps that I believe will be significantly influenced by the draw. I know from experience that unless I can eliminate at least half the runners in some way I struggle to find the winner of these competitive races often enough to make a profit. Handicaps usually attract decent-sized fields and normally one can make some sort of case for the chance of most of the runners. If you cannot eliminate at least half of them you face the confusing task of trying to weigh the pros and cons of too many contenders and it is easy to become bogged down by the mass of information at hand these days. I usually eliminate any horse that has a negative average draw figure (i.e. with an average draw figure less than 1.0). I will, however, make an exception for a confirmed front runner if I consider that it will be able to improve its track position. Obviously, the higher the draw figure a horse has the better its chance of winning.

Once the field has been narrowed down, the individual draw figures can then be used to help you decide between the contenders. At certain tracks particular stalls are strongly favoured within an 'averaged out' group and it is important to take this into account. For example, in races of between 10 and 14 furlongs at York the lowest two stalls have a significant edge over stalls three and four. If there is little to choose between a contender drawn in stall one or two and a contender drawn in stall three or four, preference should usually be given to the former. I say usually because the contender's styles of running need to be considered. If the horse drawn in stall four races prominently and the three on its inside are usually held up it will probably gain the most out of being drawn low because it will be able to move across to race against the favoured rail. It is important to consider what tactics a horse is likely to employ and how any theoretical draw advantage might be affected.

Draw figures can provide an explanation for performances that are otherwise hard to comprehend. Without them the form of most handicappers, particularly sprinters, can appear rather confusing and inconsistent because they generally run badly on the occasions they are poorly drawn and they are flattered on the occasions they are particularly well drawn. The draw figures allow you to read between the lines and appreciate the true worth of a horse's performance and they will give you an advantage over punters who do not have the same insight.

GOOD RUNS FROM POOR DRAWS

The Handicapper rarely, if at all, takes into account whether a horse was well drawn when reassessing it after a good run and a horse that wins from a good draw will usually struggle to justify a higher rating. An exposed handicapper is particularly vulnerable to an unjustified rise in its official rating and will invariably represent poor value in these circumstances. Conversely, if a horse won or ran well in spite of having had a bad draw the merit of its performance is often underestimated by the Handicapper and the horse should certainly be able to overcome at least a modest hike in its rating. These horses can be worth following and a lot of punters take a keen interest in them.

Although it is an approach that highlights plenty of future winners it is not quite the money-spinner it could be because a horse that runs well from an obviously bad draw immediately goes into most tipsters' and commentators' notebooks and will normally be well supported next time it runs. I have found that the available odds are usually too short to interest me, but I always monitor a horse's next run with interest to see whether it disappoints. If it does I will look to back it on its next outing when it may well have good prospects if conditions are favourable and there should be a better chance of obtaining value odds.

It was this approach that led me to back a good-priced winner in the shape of Antonio Canova on 28 July 2000. This horse had not been raced at two and only ran four times as a three-year-old. After his first three appearances, which came in maiden races, he was allocated an official handicap rating of 74. This qualified him to run in a 0-75 classified stakes on 8 October 1999 at York over six furlongs on good to soft ground. That day he was drawn in stall 21 of 23 (a bad draw with a figure of 0.0) and in the event his rider kept him towards the disadvantaged stands rail throughout the race. Despite this he managed to finish third, beaten only two lengths by the winner, and the merit of his performance was highlighted by the fact that he had finished six lengths ahead of the other 13 horses that had raced towards the stands side. Furthermore, Topspeed awarded the horse a speed figure of 82, which suggested that the horse was well handicapped, and of course Topspeed had not been able to take into consideration that Antonio Canova had been badly drawn! Given that he had only had four outings he was also likely to improve further.

I made a note that the horse was one to follow whenever there was some give in the ground and when he reappeared at Thirsk on 19 May 2000 my interest was heightened when I read that he had been gelded during the winter break – this often heralds improvement – and by the fact that his official rating had incredibly been lowered to 72! I did not back him at Thirsk because I felt that he might need the run, even though he was well drawn in stall 20. He ran better than I anticipated and confirmed that he retained his ability when he finished third at 12-1. He next ran at Windsor on 19 June, but I again declined to back him as the good to firm ground was against him and he did not have a good draw in stall 5 (0.78). He finished ninth and considering his promising run at Thirsk his odds of 10-1 spoke volumes about the chance he had on the ground and from his draw. At York on 15 July he ran over seven furlongs for the first time and finished eleventh after losing any chance of winning by running wide into the straight.

Following these two moderate runs the horse's official rating was dropped a further 2lbs to 70 and I was convinced that he was very well handicapped as a result. On 28 July it was finally time to strike! He was due to run in a 17-runner six-furlong handicap at Newmarket where the going was 'good', and he appeared to have a fair draw in stall 3 given that at the previous meeting the winners of the handicaps on the straight part of the course were drawn **3** (13 ran), **5** (13 ran) and **3** (16 ran). Now that he was fit and had conditions in his favour he looked ready to take advantage of what was clearly a very favourable handicap rating. The 16-1 on offer was outstanding value. He did manage to win, by just over a length. It was only my knowledge of the draw that had made me aware of the true merit of Antonio Canova's performance at York in October 1999. Without that knowledge I doubt whether I would have backed the horse at Newmarket over nine months later.

Horses that are subsequently allotted a favourable draw after running poorly from bad draws on their last one or two runs can provide excellent betting opportunities, particularly if they were previously in good form. How a horse fares when badly drawn is irrelevant because a poor run from a bad draw is excusable and it is likely to return to form as long as the prevailing conditions are favourable. If you believe that it will, you may have found a good bet. Not only will the horse's price invariably be generous following some deceptively poor performances, but as a bonus it is likely to be more favourably handicapped following a reduction of its official rating.

This is a good way to employ the draw figures because the most important aspect of winner finding is the price of the selections. Simply using the figures to highlight horses that have run well from poor draws and backing them next time they run at skinny prices is of limited value and a longer-term view needs to be adopted.

Although I firmly believe that draw figures are a crucial selection tool I recognise that they will not suit everyone. Most punters are too obsessed with being able to pick a high percentage of winners to be able to stomach the fact that on occasions the figures will eliminate obvious-looking contenders that duly win. I once gave some of my figures to a friend and I was surprised to discover that he quickly rejected them for this very reason. He couldn't seem to grasp that badly-drawn horses do win races. Choosing to ignore the statistics and backing badly-drawn horses on a regular basis is a loser's habit. Have patience and you will eventually reap the rewards of ensuring that your selections are statistically favoured by the draw as long as the rest of your method is sound!

CHAPTER FOUR

CLASS CONSCIOUS!

You will have heard commentators say things like 'that was a classy performance', or 'the horse has a touch of class'. To the uninitiated this suggests that class is a special, albeit intangible, quality. However, I suggest that class is really just another term for ability and that there is nothing intangible about it. In the same way that a horse's ability can be measured in the form of a rating so too can its class, as long as it has competed often enough and against superior opponents.

Class should not be an important factor in handicap races because the theory behind handicapping is that horses of different ability or class are afforded the same chance of winning by the different amounts of weight they carry. However, in practice weight does not have the effect on performance that it is supposed to. In line with the findings of similar research undertaken in America my analysis of all-aged handicap results from our tracks shows that class *is* a major factor. The following table is based on the results from the last five seasons.

		WINNING RATIOS	
WEIGHT CARRIED	**ALL-AGED**	**3YO ONLY**	**2YO ONLY**
9–12 – 10-00	1.35	–	–
9-9 – 9-11	1.20	–	–
9-6 – 9- 8	1.20	1.40	1.55
9-3 – 9-5	1.10	1.20	1.50
9-0 – 9-2	1.00	1.10	1.20
8-11 – 8-13	1.00	0.95	1.00
8-8 – 8-10	0.90	0.95	1.00
8-5 – 8-7	0.85	0.90	0.90
8-2 – 8-4	0.80	0.80	0.80
7-13 – 8-1	0.75	0.70	0.60
7-10 – 7-12	0.60	0.60	0.50
7-7 – 7-9	0.50	0.40	0.30

If the existing handicap scale and weight were effective as tools for levelling ability then the distribution of winners to runners would be equally spread between the various weight bands. However, as the table shows the top-weighted horses in all-aged handicaps win nearly three times as often as the bottom-weighted horses and in nurseries they win more than five times as often. Although the win ratios of the bottom weight band are dragged down to some extent by the fact that they include horses disadvantaged by running from long-handicap marks, the table proves that class does have a major determining effect on the outcome of handicaps. The horses at the top end of the weights are, in the Handicapper's view, the best in the race and despite having to concede weight to their slower rivals they are able to make their superior ability tell far more often than they should do according to the theory.

There are, however, certain circumstances under which weight can have a greater or lesser effect on class than the overall figures in the table indicate. As a rule the effect of weight on class is determined by how fast a race is run, particularly in the early stages. The faster the pace the more effect weight has on a horse's performance. Sharp bends and surface undulations slow horses down and courses with these characteristics tend to suit the higher-weighted horses. Galloping tracks with flat surfaces and long sweeping turns, such as Newmarket and Doncaster, negate their advantage to some extent because they encourage truly-run races that enhance the effect of weight.

The following table shows the impact that tight bends have on class. It compares the results from Newmarket, which is a wide galloping track with only one relatively insignificant bend and a stiff uphill finish, to the results from Ripon which is a narrower track with surface undulations and two tight bends.

AVERAGE NUMBER OF WINNERS FROM EVERY 100 RACES			
	7-7 – 8-4	8-5 – 9-2	9-3 – 10-0
NEWMARKET	27	35.5	37.5
RIPON	19	32	49

The highest weight band wins 39% more often than the lowest weight band in races run at Newmarket, but at Ripon that superiority increases to 158% and the large difference between the two demonstrates how course characteristics can alter the influence of weight.

There is one notable exception that proves the rule and that is Chester. It would be reasonable to anticipate that the class horses have a big advantage at Chester given that races there are run almost continuously on the turn, but surprisingly this is not the case as the following table shows.

AVERAGE NUMBER OF WINNERS FROM EVERY 100 RACES			
	7-7 – 8-4	8-5 – 9-2	9-3 – 10-0
CHESTER	31	36	33

After looking at some recordings of races run at Chester, I concluded that the main reason for this anomaly is probably the draw factor. Because it is a big advantage to hold a low draw and to maintain a prominent position during a race, the jockeys drawn near the inside rail tend to set off at a fast pace in order not to relinquish that advantage. The well-cambered turns and flat surface allow the runners to maintain such a strong gallop that weight has a greater effect on the class horses than is normal at other tight tracks.

The effect that a strong gallop has on a horse's ability to carry weight, particularly on straight courses where the runners are not slowed down by bends, is best illustrated by the results of some of the season's major handicaps such as the Cambridgeshire and the Royal Hunt Cup. These races which attract huge fields are invariably run at a furious pace, and the ten-year trends show that horses carrying over nine stone have a relatively poor record and are usually worth opposing. The table below draws a comparison between a selection of large-field handicaps that are run on straight galloping courses and other handicaps that either have smaller fields or include two or more bends. It shows the average winning weight of the winners from the last eleven years and it demonstrates how a strong gallop increases the influence that weight has on the outcome of a race.

RACE TITLE	DISTANCE	COURSE	AVERAGE WEIGHT CARRIED BY THE WINNER
CESAREWITCH (ONE BEND)	18F	NEWMARKET	8-5
CAMBRIDGESHIRE	9F	NEWMARKET	8-8
WOKINGHAM	6F	ASCOT	8-10
ROYAL HUNT CUP	8F	ASCOT	8-5
ASCOT STAKES (HANDICAP)	20F	ASCOT	9-1
THIRSK HANDICAP ON TUESDAY OF ROYAL ASCOT	7F	THIRSK	9-2
RIPON HANDICAP ON THURSDAY OF ROYAL ASCOT	5F	RIPON	9-5

Note that the Ascot Stakes favours the top-weights despite being a competitive big-field handicap and that there is a marked difference between it and the two races run over Ascot's straight course. There is also a significant difference between the record of the top-weights in the Cesarewitch and the Ascot Stakes, despite the fact that they are run over similar distances and have a similar number of runners. Clearly the sharp nature of the turns in the long-distance races at Ascot reduces the impact of weight, which is probably because they slow the runners down and allow them to take a 'breather' during a race. The handicaps at Ripon and Thirsk are comparatively uncompetitive affairs that attract far fewer runners than the other races in the example. They are seldom run at such a strong gallop and both the slightly undulating surfaces and Thirsk's tight bend help to slow the runners down. These characteristics clearly favour the top-weights and the extra pounds they carry do not have the impact on performance that they are supposed to.

Another factor that has an influence on the effect of weight is the going. Although proper analysis of the effect heavy or soft ground has on the influence of weight is difficult because there is limited data on which to draw, my figures suggest that very soft ground does reduce the advantage held by the horses at the top of the handicap, but that the impact is often overstated. On those occasions when a strong pace is guaranteed and the going is very soft the top weights will invariably struggle, but in slowly-run races at favourable tracks they are still able to dominate.

Because weight does not have the effect it is supposed to and because runners carrying over nine stone have a distinct advantage at most tracks it follows that horses dropping in class from one race to another have a better chance of winning than those rising in class. In order to prove this I took 1,000 examples of horses that had either won or finished within one length of the winner in a handicap and recorded how they fared on their next handicap outing. This was the result:

	DOWN IN CLASS	SAME CLASS	UP IN CLASS
	WHERE THE TOP RATED HORSE WAS RATED 7LBS OR MORE BELOW THE TOP RATED HORSE IN THE QUALIFYING RACE		WHERE THE TOP RATED HORSE WAS RATED 7 LBS OR MORE HIGHER THAN THE TOP RATED HORSE IN THE QUALIFYING RACE
NUMBER OF RUNNERS	176	274	550
NUMBER OF WINNERS	58	63	94
PERCENTAGE OF WINNERS	33 %	23 %	17 %

These statistics reinforce the argument that weight does not have the effect it is supposed to for they show that horses dropped in class win twice as often as a percentage of runners than those that are raised in grade. In theory this should not be the case, for in handicaps the difficulty of rising in class is supposed to be negated by the fact that a horse carries less weight as it moves up in grade.

Rather surprisingly, the table also shows that trainers are three times more likely to raise their in-form horses in class than to lower them. There are occasions when the trainer has no choice. For example, if a horse wins a 0-70 handicap when rated 70 it must move up in class because the inevitable upward revision of its official rating will exclude it from future 0-70 events. However, this does not explain why so many trainers decide against finding the easiest winning opportunity for their in-form horses.

I think there are two other explanations for this anomaly. The first is prize money. As a rule the higher the class of handicap the greater the prize money and it is not surprising that connections are tempted to aim for the bigger pot, for as trainer Noel Chance once said: 'I like nothing better than going through the programme book making plans and dreams. You don't make money out of training horses, you make it out of winning big races. When you stop winning the big ones, you're in trouble.'

The second reason is that a lot of people in racing who should know better still believe that the more weight a horse carries in a handicap the less chance it has of winning and they seem to have no understanding of the impact class has in these races. When connections are interviewed they often say things like: 'He had a lot of weight to carry that day', or when referring to a runner set to carry say 7-12: 'She's at the right end of the handicap.'

BACK HORSES IN THEIR RIGHT CLASS

Although most trainers opt to go for the bigger prize money offered by the higher-class races there are others who aim to win as many races as possible and they try to achieve this by placing their horses, more often than not, in a suitable class of race. Perhaps the most obvious of these is Martin Pipe whose National Hunt horses frequently rattle up sequences in low-grade races. One of the keys to Pipe's remarkable record-breaking seasonal tallies is his awareness of class. Roy Hawkins, who worked for Pipe as a form adviser, cast some light onto the Pipe team's thinking when he once said: 'Backing or running horses in their own class, or preferably below it, dramatically reduces the odds against defeat.' If you wish to improve your chances of success as a punter you would do well to take a leaf out of the Pipe team's book and concentrate on horses that are competing in or below their class!

Exposed handicappers, particularly those rated 80 or below, are very susceptible to changes in class and they often have an identifiable level above which they become noticeably ineffectual. When you look at a horse's career record, particularly that of an older horse, you will often see that all or most of its wins have been achieved below a certain class level and that the horse has a definite class ceiling. For example, take the record of seven-year-old gelding Cauda Equina before he ran on 4 June 2001. The *Racing Post* form guide showed that all of his eleven wins had been in 0-80 races or lower which suggested that the gelding was ineffectual in races above that level. Further analysis of past form books revealed this was the case and that Cauda Equina had competed in races of a higher grade than 0-80 on 48 occasions, but had no wins and just seven placings to his credit is a dismal record. However, he had competed in 0-80 races or below on 41 occasions and had recorded an impressive eleven wins (a strike rate of 27%) and eleven places. His record showed that he was frequently 'outpaced' in the higher grades, but when he competed below his class ceiling he was very effective and worth following closely, particularly on good ground.

Another typical example is provided by Topton. On 9 June 2001 he was due to run in a 0-80 handicap at Doncaster. The *Racing Post* showed that all of his six wins on turf had been in races of 0-80 or below. A study of past form books confirmed that he had a definite class ceiling and that he was ineffectual in races of a higher grade than 0-80. He had competed above that level on 28 occasions but had managed only four placings. However, his record below that level was very good for an exposed handicapper. From 29 runs he had managed six wins (21%) and ten places and he was very consistent when running in the appropriate class. Last time out Topton had signalled his well-being by coming second in a 0-85 race at Newbury. He had now been dropped back to his right level and had the added advantage of a favourable high draw. Not surprisingly, with the prevailing conditions in his favour, he duly improved his record in the lower grade to seven wins from 30 starts and landed some nice bets in the process.

A low-grade handicapper that is not obviously improving will invariably have a class ceiling and it is well worth taking the trouble to look through past form books to identify it and to make a note of it for future reference. Not only will such research help you to identify the grade that a horse is most likely to win in but, just as importantly, you will know when it can be confidently eliminated.

Class ceilings are not usually as apparent from the *Racing Post* form summaries as the two examples I have given. Horses occasionally win uncompetitive races that are theoretically above their class ceiling if they are well-handicapped and favoured by the prevailing conditions; this can give a false impression to the casual observer. Just because a horse wins a race in the higher grade does not mean that it has suddenly become fully effective at that level. If, for example, Cauda Equina should finally scrape home in a 0-90 event his record in races above his class ceiling will still read very poorly in comparison to his record in 0-80 events or below! The win does not change the fact that he is ineffectual in the higher grades and that he should be opposed remorselessly when running in such events. It is, however, easy to be deceived by such a win unless you do the research to establish how a horse has performed in the different levels of class. The table below helps to explain why class ceilings exist. It shows the average number of seconds per mile that each grade of handicap is run slower than the 'standard time'.

HANDICAP GRADE	SECONDS PER MILE BEHIND STANDARD	AVERAGE NUMBER OF BEHIND A 0-115 HANDICAP
0 – 115	2.5	–
0 – 110	2.9	2.3L
0 – 100	3.3	4.7L
0 – 90	3.9	8.2L
0 – 80	4.3	10.5L
0 – 70	4.9	14.1L
0 – 60	5.5	17.6L

Although the table over-simplifies things, it nevertheless demonstrates that when a horse is raised in class it normally has to run faster in order to remain competitive. Improving horses raised in class might prove to have the necessary speed and stamina but fully exposed ones will usually struggle unless the effect of weight is enhanced by the track, the number of runners, or extremely testing ground. When assessing a race I eliminate an exposed horse if it has been raised in class to a grade in which it has not previously won. Although this type of horse will sometimes appear to run well in the higher class it will almost invariably find at least one opponent too good.

In most instances then, concentrating on the class horses in a race will subtly shift the odds of success in your favour. As a rule it is unwise to select a horse that is carrying less than eight stone but obviously the available odds will determine whether it is worth risking a bet or not. It is important to be flexible and to remember that at certain racetracks and under certain conditions the bottom weights are not necessarily at a disadvantage.

When available, it is always worth checking the 'Ten-Year Trends' and 'Reverse Trends' features in the *Racing Post* and *Raceform on Saturday* for clues, particularly for the big handicaps. You also need to remember to take 'weight-for-age' into consideration when assessing the class of three-year-olds running in all-aged handicaps and to add the appropriate allowance back onto the weight they are set to carry.

In addition to the more obvious culprits for a poor performance such as the draw, going and distance, the impact of class needs to be considered. You should expect hand-icappers to perform disappointingly when carrying a low weight and be prepared to ignore a poor run in such circumstances. Those that manage to win when carrying a low weight will often be worth following, particularly if they are lightly raced with scope for improvement. Do not expect an exposed horse that is raised in class after running well under a big weight to reproduce that level of form; this type of horse should normally be opposed. If you go through the records of handicappers you will find that it is quite common for them to win, then to lose when raised to a higher grade, only to win again next time out when dropped back in class.

Topton again provides a good example. On 15 July 1999 he won a 0-75 handicap by over two lengths, going clear in the final furlong to win easily. On his next outing, possibly due to the ease of his victory, his trainer decided to raise him in class to a 0-100 handicap at Newmarket where he ran on to finish fourth, having typically been 'outpaced over a furlong out' by his faster opponents. Following that good run he was dropped back down in class to a handicap at Yarmouth in which he was the highest-rated horse on a mark of 74. The best of the opposition was rated just 65 which meant that he was taking a 35lbs drop in class, and not surprisingly he was able to return to the winner's enclosure.

Although the statistics show that it is best to avoid exposed handicappers that are raised in class following a win, a lightly-raced horse that is in winning form, or any horse that has yet to show its true ability, will often be able to overcome a rise in class. This type of horse may have a handicap rating that does not reflect its ultimate true potential because it is still maturing and improving, or its trainer may only just have found the key to unlocking its ability.

When an improving, or 'momentum' horse, begins a winning roll it will take rises in class in its stride until its rating is raised to a level that reflects its true ability. A good recent example of this type of horse is Brevity. It was not until the horse joined his fourth trainer, the excellent Milton Bradley, that his potential was finally unlocked. Now a six-year-old, the gelding had only won one previous race from 22 starts, off an official rating of just 49. He started the 2001 season on a mark of 55 but went on to win eight races, taking several rises in class in his stride. On his final start, he was beaten a neck in the Ayr Gold Cup off a rating of 96.

Occasionally an old, exposed handicapper will run up a winning sequence and overcome rises in class in the process. However, in most instances it will simply be recapturing its old sparkle following a sustained loss of form and returning to a level reached in a previous season. It is normal for the run to peter out once the horse's handicap rating returns to around its previous high. When this type of horse returns to winning form look to see what rating it has achieved in the past as a guide to what it might achieve again in the future. Be alert to factors that might signal a return to that level, such as a change of trainer or a successful medical operation.

Brecongill Lad is a good example of this type of horse. Prior to joining the stable of David Nicholls halfway through the 1999 season his form had gradually deteriorated and his official rating had dropped from a high of 79 down to a lowly 50. He was clearly potentially well handicapped if his new handler could bring about a return to form and not surprisingly, given Nicholls' ability to rejuvenate horses, Brecongill Lad began by winning two 0-65 handicaps for his new yard. He was then stepped up in class to a 0-90 handicap and won off a rating of 62 and two races later he went on to win a 0-95 handicap when rated 68. When Brecongill Lad joined Nicholls he was seven years old, he had already run 41 times, he was fully exposed and he was very unlikely to improve upon what he had achieved in the past. It was only because he had already proven himself in the higher class prior to his recent decline in form, and because he had joined a new stable with a record of rejuvenating horses, that he could have been considered as a possible bet when repeatedly raised in class by his new connections.

CHAPTER FIVE

THE SELECTION PROCESS

Before discussing how the selection process works in practice we should firstly consider how best to approach the business of searching through the day's form for suitable betting opportunities.

A common mistake made by punters is that they analyse too many races and do not delve deeply enough into them. They prefer to flit through as many races as possible looking for probable winners and they believe that the more selections they make the more likely they are to win. They tend to spread their available funds over a number of selections and a variety of bets instead of putting larger amounts on just one or two horses because they feel that they are more likely to have a winner. They want the action of being involved in as many races as possible.

It is imperative to be more selective than your average punter and I recommend that you concentrate on a maximum of two handicaps per day. I know from experience that whenever I attempt to analyse more than two races I struggle to fit all the necessary analysis into the morning and I become prone to oversights and silly mistakes.

It is worth spending a little time deciding which race or races are most likely to repay in-depth analysis. There are a number of factors to consider. Obviously, if you are using a bias-orientated method, it is sensible to concentrate on those races most likely to be determined by them and the draw and pace charts contained in this book will highlight these. Another important consideration is class. Be wary of big-field handicaps in which virtually all the runners are carrying over nine stone. All the runners are of a similar class and the race is therefore likely to be more competitive than one in which the runners are carrying from ten stone down to eight stone or below. It is also sensible to concentrate on the higher-class handicaps where possible.

Although the only rule I have is to try to avoid saddling myself with inflexible rules, I am cautious of getting involved in handicaps below the class level of 0-80. That is unless the draw bias is so pronounced that it is possible to quickly narrow the field down to just a few contenders. Handicaps below this level are full of types that cannot be relied on, and they are best avoided. The number of runners is another factor to consider. Because a lot of my bets are placed each way on outsiders I tend to concentrate on races which have 16 or more runners. Not only does this mean that I collect if my selection finishes fourth, but, according to Peter May, the author of *Forecasting Methods For Horseracing*, when there are between 16 and 25 runners the current fraction of one quarter the odds for the place portion of the bet is higher than the theoretically fair fraction and therefore offers a degree of value.

NARROWING THE FIELD DOWN

Once a decision has been taken about which races to concentrate on, the next step is to narrow the field down to the logical contenders through a process of elimination. I recommend that you begin by putting a line through the runners which have negative average draw figures – in other words **0.9** or below. Although it may seem dubious to eliminate the runners that are only marginally encumbered, the idea is to concentrate on the horses that are afforded a distinct edge by their stall position and basically the higher the draw figure the better. There will, however, be occasions when a horse with a negative figure appears to have an outstanding chance for other reasons and you can afford to be flexible as long as you do not stray too far below **1.0**.

To guard against your selection being outclassed the runners that are officially rated 20lbs or more below the top-rated horse in the handicap should be eliminated. You can make an exception if the ten-year trends for a major handicap suggest the lower weights are favoured, or if you identify that a horse below the cut-off level looks to have been underrated and should in fact be above it. Usually the horse in question will be a lightly-raced type or a horse that has begun to recapture its old form following a significant drop in its official rating. There are also a number of tracks such as Chester and Newmarket where the advantage held by the top-weights is either reduced or negated.

Having worked out the pace figures for the race you will usually be able to eliminate some of the remaining contenders on the grounds that their particular style of running will put them at a disadvantage at the track in question, or because the race is unlikely to unfold in their favour. The headings below can then be used to reduce the number of contenders further.

Is the Horse Blinkered or Visored for the First Time?

A horse that is wearing blinkers or a visor for the first time, and has not previously been equipped with either type, is unlikely to win. Most horses get far too upset the first time they wear the headgear at the track and they run too freely to reproduce their best form. You will have heard television pundits state on numerous occasions that the application of the headgear is a positive factor. Ignore them! Statistics show that horses blinkered or visored for the first time win approximately half as often as normal and they should be eliminated.

How Old Is the Horse?

John McCririck often advises punters not to back a three-year-old against older horses in a handicap before June and for once he is right! Three-year-olds are not mature enough to compete effectively against older horses during the first few months of the season and the current weight-for-age scale does not compensate them enough for their immaturity. Although they start to become competitive against their elders in June it is only in the final two months of the season that the weight-for-age scale affords them parity with older horses. The chart below has been compiled from the results of all-aged handicaps taken from two seasons and it gives the win ratios of the various age groups, showing how they alter as the season unfolds:

AGE	MARCH – MAY	JUNE – JULY	AUGUST – SEPTEMBER	OCTOBER – NOVEMBER	TOTAL
3YO	0.5	0.9	0.8	1.0	0.8
4YO	0.8	0.9	1.1	1.1	1.0
5YO	1.5	1.2	1.3	1.3	1.3
6YO	1.2	0.9	1.0	0.9	1.0
7YO, 8YO	0.8	1.1	0.9	1.0	0.95
9YO+	0.7	0.7	0.6	0.4	0.6

The three-year-olds are at a big disadvantage during the first few months of the year and they can be eliminated when competing against older horses. If a three-year-old wins or performs with credit in an all-aged handicap before June it is usually worth following, particularly if it subsequently returns to a handicap restricted to its own age group.

If you look at the weight-for-age scale you will see that during the early months of the season four-year-olds receive an allowance from their elders in races of nine furlongs or further and this reflects the fact that they have not yet reached full maturity. It is not until halfway through July that they are deemed to be the equal of their elders at all distances. The table above supports the official view, but it also proves that four-year-olds are at a disadvantage during the first few months of the Turf season, irre-spective of any allowance they receive. In fact, the table provides further proof if you need it, that weight does not have the effect it is supposed to. Three-year-olds receive big weight allowances from their elders, particularly during the first few months of the season, but as the chart shows, in spite of this, they are still unable to compete effectively against them.

The table also confirms that horses do not reach full maturity until the age of five. Five-year-olds have a significant edge over the other age groups, especially during the first few months of the season when they make the most of the immaturity of their juniors. It is certainly worth paying extra attention to them, particularly as the odds compilers appear to ignore this strong bias. By the time horses reach the age of six they are usually fully exposed and the Handicapper invariably has their measure. This explains why horses between the age of six and eight have an inferior record to the five-year-olds, for they are certainly not too old and are in fact probably physically stronger. Indeed, when I was compiling the data for the above chart, I noted that the majority of races restricted to amateur riders are won by horses aged six or over. There is little doubt that their superior strength means they are better able to cope with the bigger weights carried in these races than their less-mature rivals.

Horses begin to lose their speed fairly quickly when they reach the age of nine and their win ratio declines sharply. Although you will occasionally come across multiple winners such as the nine-year-old Nineacres (who won nine races during the 2000 season), they are rare. As a rule, horses of this age are on the downgrade and they should be avoided. I put a line through horses that are aged ten or older and in the ultra-competitive major handicaps I eliminate anything aged eight or over.

Is the Horse Fit Enough to Reproduce its Best Form?

When I first started betting this was normally an easy question to answer. If a horse had not run for about six weeks or more it was likely to need its first run back at the track to reach peak fitness. These days, thanks to the influence of Martin Pipe and one or two other trainers, a lot more horses are trained sufficiently hard at home to be fit come race day. Nevertheless, if a horse has been absent from the track for a long period, particularly if it is having its first run of the season, it is worth checking both its record to see how it fared on similar occasions in the past and the trainer's record with first-time-out runners for clues. Unless these give cause for encouragement the horse should be eliminated.

There are, however, some horses that only reproduce their best form after they have had a break from the track. Usually they are only at their best on their first one or two runs of the season, or after a lengthy mid-season break (two months or more). It is worth getting to know these horses as they often start at generous odds given that most punters write them off on the grounds that they will be unfit following their absence.

If you identify one that is returning from a break you can be confident that if conditions are favourable it will run a big race. A good example is Marsad. He won his first race of the season in both 1998 and 1999 and in 2000 he finished a creditable fifth of 18 when badly drawn at Kempton. After that Kempton run he performed moderately on each of his next three outings before being given a 94-day break. He reappeared at Goodwood on 26 August 2000 and his long absence from the track should have alerted punters to the likelihood that he would reproduce his best form. His chance that day was enhanced by a good draw in stall 18 and by the fact that he was well handicapped. His poor run of form had resulted in his official rating dropping 6lbs to 86 since the beginning of the season and that looked lenient given that he had clocked Topspeed figures of 101 and 100 in 1999. The horse was on offer at a generous-looking 25-1 in the morning and in a 21-runner field he looked excellent each-way value. In the event he finished a good second but was unable to cope with the well-handicapped Surprise.

Is the Horse Suited by the Going?

I will not bore you with a long-winded explanation of something that you are doubtless au fait with. Suffice to say that if a horse is clearly unsuited to the prevailing going it should be eliminated. The *Racing Post's* form guide furnishes you with all the relevant information, for it shows how many times each horse has won, placed and run on the going. If the flat going has altered since the paper went to press you might have to plough through some form books to get the necessary information! Be wary of paying too much heed to a horse's early form when assessing going preferences because a two- or three-year-old will win a maiden or other low-grade race in spite of the going, simply because it outclassed the opposition. A recent handicap win is the best guide. One of the reasons why I prefer to concentrate on decent-class handicaps is that the better hand-icappers can be confidently eliminated if their record shows that they are unsuited to the going. However, low-grade handicappers often seem to buck their own trends and win despite apparently not being favoured by the prevailing conditions.

Is the Horse Suited by the Distance of the Race?

Again this does not merit much explanation for a horse's distance preferences are normally apparent and usually there is only doubt when a lightly-raced horse is stepped up in trip. Most of the information you need can be found in the *Racing Post*. The paper's form guide gives the median winning distance of the horse's sire's offspring and this is a pretty good guide to a horse's suitability for a particular distance. Lawrence Taylor's book *Form Sires* is another useful source of information that you can turn to for clues.

Trainers often campaign their lightly-raced three-year-olds over inadequate trips with the intention of getting them well handicapped. When they are subsequently tried over longer distances they frequently show improved form and prove to be leniently treated. A lot of the major handicaps are farmed by the big trainers in this way and it pays to watch out for lightly-raced horses that are stepping up in trip to a distance that their breeding suggests they will be suited to.

Before deciding if a horse will be suited to the distance of a particular race it is necessary to consider what emphasis the race will place on stamina. There are four factors to consider – the number of runners, the number of front runners, the course and the going. As a rule, the more runners there are the stronger the pace will be and the stronger the pace the greater the need for stamina becomes. This explains why the major handicaps tend to be won either by horses that have won over a longer distance in the past, or those that have previously run well in a similar race (despite this fact I didn't see Tayseer coming in the 2000 Stewards' Cup!).

In comparison, the pace in small fields is usually modest and there is rarely a premium on stamina unless several front runners force the early pace. The stiffness of the track also has an influence on the stamina requirement, as does the prevailing going, and the softer the ground the greater the need for stamina becomes. As you will see in the chapter *The Theory in Practice* (see page 81), it was this line of thinking that led me to back Lady Boxer at 33-1 in the six-furlong Ayr Silver Cup in 2000.

Is the Horse Well Enough Handicapped to Win?

The next stage is to determine which of the remaining contenders are well enough handicapped to win the race and to eliminate those that are not. It is a fact that a horse's chance of winning is determined by its official rating. If its rating is too high it has virtually no chance of winning a competitive handicap, even if other factors such as the draw and the ground are in its favour. More often than not there will be at least one better-handicapped horse that proves too strong for it.

There are two reasons why a horse's handicap rating has such an influence on its chance of winning. Firstly, it determines how much weight a horse carries in relation to its rivals, but secondly and more importantly, it decides what class of race a horse can compete in. For example, if a horse's rating is raised from 65 to 76 it can no longer compete in 0-75 handicaps or below; it has to take on better-class opposition in 0-80 handicaps or above. Horses win most frequently when they give weight away to inferior opponents and when they are forced to step up in class they struggle unless they are improving. When a horse's rating rises to a certain level, not only will it lack the necessary finishing speed to cope with the faster rivals it is forced to compete against, but it will have to carry too much weight in relation to them. This 'double whammy' invariably proves too difficult to overcome.

This relationship between a horse's official rating, class and weight is perfectly illustrated by the career of the ten-year-old gelding Mousehole. Mousehole cannot win if his rating is raised above 70 and he finds it hard to win when competing in any handicap or stakes race of a higher class than 0-70. He has run off a rating higher than 70 on 27 occasions and has failed to record a single win. However, when rated 70 or below his record is more impressive for he has won twelve out of 50 races. His record is even better if class is taken into account. He has run in 0-70 events on 21 occasions and has won ten of them – an outstanding 48% strike rate that is a credit to the horse's consistency when he is well handicapped and running in his correct class.

Mousehole struggles when competing in a class higher than 0-70 and has managed only two wins in 53 attempts. The first win came during 2000 when he sneaked home by a neck when well drawn at Sandown in a 0-80 race and the second came in an uncompetitive-looking 0-85 handicap at Nottingham on 11 June 2001, when he again won by a narrow margin. Those wins came when he was officially rated 66 and 65, several pounds below his highest winning rating of 69, and I suspect that it was this fact that enabled him to scramble home. Whenever Mousehole is rated above 70 he finds the double-whammy of competing against opponents rated 75 or higher, and having to carry several pounds too many in relation to them, too much to cope with.

So how do you tell if a horse is well handicapped or not? My preferred way is to use form and speed ratings that are based on the official handicap scale for they allow a direct comparison to be made between the rating awarded to a horse and the horse's official handicap mark. I have found the ratings produced by Postmark and Topspeed to be good, particularly the latter. Although they have the advantage of being based on the official scale, their ratings do seem to have drifted upwards by several pounds over time and for now at least they need adjusting. Last season I was of the opinion that they were seven pounds too high in relation to the official scale and I deducted that amount from them. Timeform's figures are also based on the official scale and they have a good reputation.

I prefer to rely on speed figures rather than form ratings because I believe that they provide a more useful measurement of the value of a horse's performance. Form figures such as those produced by Postmark are devalued by the fact that the winner of a handicap automatically attracts a rating higher than its official handicap mark. Of course on many occasions the winner will have shown improved form, but there are numerous races when this is not the case and the winner is simply the best of a bad or out-of-form bunch. There has to be a winner of every handicap but a good proportion of them do not deserve to have their rating automatically increased.

The speed figures produced by Topspeed or Timeform do not have this inherent weakness. On many occasions the ratings awarded to the winner of a handicap will be lower than the horse's official rating and they are thus able to differentiate between good and poor form. Although the form of a slowly-run race is not necessarily suspect, a slow time can reflect that a race was relatively uncompetitive and the winner may not have needed to show improved form to win. The winner of an uncompetitive race may not deserve an upward revision of its rating; exposed handicappers in particular will usually struggle to win again off an unjustified higher mark. If on the other hand the winner attracts a speed figure higher than its official rating the form is likely to be solid and it is reasonable to conclude that the horse has shown improvement.

Beware Conditions Race Form

The relationship between slowly-run races and suspect form is particularly apparent in the results of Conditions races, which often bring horses of widely different abilities together on similar weight terms. It is surprising how many exposed horses appear to show improvement in this type of race, only to flop on their return to handicaps when seemingly well treated. How, for example, did Demolition Jo appear to run so well in a Listed race on 6 August 2000 when she was officially rated a modest 72? She was unlikely to be improving because she had already raced 63 times and she was clearly outclassed in the company of horses rated 115, 108, 107, 104 and 103. However, she managed to finish only two and a half lengths behind the winner, only three-quarters of a length behind the horses rated 108 and 107 and ahead of the horse rated 115! Postmark understandably reacted by awarding Demolition Jo a rating of 88, but did she deserve it? On the face of it she had shown improved form, but the true value of her finishing position was called into question by the time of the race. Significantly Topspeed awarded the horse a rating of only 51, 21lbs *lower* than her official handicap mark, and this suggested that Demolition Jo had simply been flattered by a falsely-run race.

The Handicapper took a more realistic view of the horse's run than Postmark and he did not raise Demolition Jo's official rating. The mare raced a further three times during 2000 but failed to win, even though her official rating was lowered to just 70 later in the season, and she obviously had not improved. Be wary of accepting a seemingly improved performance from a horse at face value unless it attracted a speed figure significantly higher than its official rating. If the horse in question is fully exposed any apparent sudden improvement is suspicious, irrespective of the speed figure, unless you can identify a sound reason why it might have progressed such as a successful operation or a change of handler.

If a horse clocks a Topspeed figure seven pounds or more higher than its current official rating it is certainly well-handicapped and is very likely to win again. When you come across a horse that boasts such a Topspeed figure it is worth checking to ensure that the qualifying race was not overrated. I have found that runners in races open to amateur riders often attract high figures and it seems that for whatever reason the higher weight scale used in these events artificially inflates the ratings. Occasionally a race is overrated for no obvious reason and you need to guard against accepting such figures at face value.

For example race 3473 in the *Racing Post* 1999 Flat Form Book (3956 in *Raceform*) had clearly been overrated. The first 23 runners home were awarded Topspeed figures higher than their official ratings, but it is extremely unlikely that such a high proportion of the runners would have shown improved form. I become suspicious if more than the first four home are awarded figures higher than their official ratings, although the number of runners in the race and how exposed the horses were that attracted the high figures should be taken into account.

The other method I favour for determining if a horse is well handicapped is to simply compare its highest previous winning rating to its current one. This is easy to do because the *Racing Post* form guide prints the horse's official rating alongside each previous handicap win. The horse can almost certainly win another handicap when running off the same rating or lower, unless it has deteriorated due to injury or some other reason. If the win was achieved in either the current or the preceding season and the horse has not subsequently been absent for a lengthy period (often a sign of an injury) the rating can be taken at face value. But if the win occurred two or more seasons ago it is often worthless.

I use ratings to determine whether a horse can win a handicap off its current rating, *not* whether it is sufficiently well handicapped in *relation to* its rivals to win the race I am analysing. This is an important distinction to make. The question of how well weighted a horse is in relation to its rivals is often determined by factors such as the draw, going and class and it is not possible to weigh their effect in pounds. It does not matter how well weighted a horse is in theory, if these factors are against it will struggle to win, no matter what the handicap 'experts' would have you believe.

Medicean's run in the 2000 John Smith's Cup at York demonstrates this point. The colt had managed to finish only one length behind Giant's Causeway at level weights in the Group One St James's Palace Stakes on 20 June 2000. On the face of it that was excellent form and the official handicapper reacted by raising Medicean's rating by 15lbs. However, the John Smith's Cup – formerly the Magnet Cup – is an early-closing race and the colt was able to race off his old mark. Most of the media pundits considered that he was a certainty. He was sent off a warm 5-2 favourite in a 21-runner field, but his supporters were guilty of putting weight, form and ratings ahead of the fact that the horse had an appalling draw in stall 21 (draw figure **0.3**). In reality the horse was *badly* handicapped as a result of the race conditions and he should have been opposed with a low-drawn horse at a bigger price.

After the race his jockey Pat Eddery reported: 'I had no chance from the draw, which was a killer. I was wide and could never get in – the horse was on his wrong leg all the way round the turn and in the straight I just had too much ground to make up. In the end I just had to accept it.' The first eight home in the race were drawn 8, 3, 11, 5, 9, 4, 2 and 1 and the theoretical question of how well handicapped the horses drawn in stalls 12 to 22 were was irrelevant. Like most of these so-called 'handicap snips' Medicean was sent off at ludicrously short odds because every man and his dog wanted to be on it – a case of the blind leading the blind!

The fact that Medicean had been well handicapped if only he had been well drawn was confirmed by his next run. He returned to Group One company in the Sussex Stakes at Goodwood and once again raced against Giant's Causeway at level weights. The result was much as before with Medicean finishing just over two lengths behind Giant's Causeway, confirming that he **was** an improved performer and that he had justified the 15lbs rise in his official rating.

The hardest horses to assess are lightly-raced three- and four-year-olds. The Handicapper has limited evidence to draw on when assigning this type a rating and the official ratings are relatively unreliable. Given that they have the scope to improve upon what they have already shown on the racecourse, it is not particularly satisfactory simply to rely on the ratings they have been awarded as a guide to whether they are well handicapped. Further analysis is required. I pay particular attention to a horse if it has had five or fewer outings and I pose the following questions to decide whether or not it has been underrated:

What was the horse's starting price when it first ran?

The initial SP is a good indicator of how the horse is regarded by connections, but you have to make allowances for who the trainer is. Henry Cecil's runners, for example, invariably have an SP that is artificially short.

Who is the horse's owner and what is its breeding?

The big owners, particularly the Arabs, buy or breed the best horses, not many of which finish their careers competing in lowly handicaps. Improvement should be anticipated from most of their lightly-raced horses.

Who is the trainer?

Certain Trainers such as Dunlop, Prescott, Cecil and Stoute specialise in harvesting big handicaps with lightly-raced and underrated horses, but this is normally anticipated by the bookies.

What distance has the horse been running over so far?

One of the simplest ways to disguise a horse's true ability is to run it over either too long, or too short a trip. Check the horse's breeding in the *Racing Post* and the median winning distance of the sire's progeny for clues. Improved form shown by a lightly-raced horse often coincides with a switch to a more suitable distance.

What ratings has the horse been awarded by either Timeform or Topspeed?

If they have awarded the horse a rating higher than its official handicap mark the latter may prove to be lenient.

What is the horse's style of running?

Horses that try to lead or race prominently are easier for the handicapper to evaluate than those that are held up in the rear or mid-division for a late run. If a horse comes from behind to win without having been put under pressure, it is harder to judge just how much it had in hand.

Has the horse only been ridden by inexperienced riders to date, particularly 7lb claimers?

It will often show improved form when a jockey takes over.

Has the horse been poorly drawn on a number of occasions in the past?

If so it is probably underrated.

In the chapter *The Theory in Practice* (see page 65) you will see how I used other information in addition to the above to identify that Strong Presence had been underrated by the Handicapper before his handicap debut after three previous runs. It is not my intention to lay down a set of strict rules for you to follow because there is always room for intuition and a bit of lateral thinking!

What Is the Horse's Wins to Runs Record?

Horses that have a poor wins to runs record should be avoided. It does not matter how much a horse has in its favour before a race, if it does not try very hard or is woefully one-paced in a finish, it is unlikely to win. A horse's wins to runs record is a good indicator of its ability and courage and it is worth taking the time to work out each runner's strike rate.

What importance you should attach to a horse's strike rate depends on how many times it has run. If it has run say 30 times or more and has a wins to runs record of 5% or less it clearly either lacks the determination to win, or struggles because it is one-paced and it is unlikely that its strike rate will ever significantly improve. Bearing in mind that it wins only one race in 20 you do not want to take a short price about it!

When assessing a horse's strike rate it is important to take class into account. As the example of Mousehole demonstrates it is common for a horse to have a good strike rate when competing in a low class but a dismal one when competing in a higher grade. If a horse has spent much of its career competing out of its depth its overall strike rate will be artificially depressed and can often mask an excellent record in a lower class. The number of times a horse has run also needs to be considered as does its age. Lightly raced three- and four-year-old maidens should not be eliminated just because they are yet to win a race for they have scope to improve, particularly if they have not had many runs over their preferred distance. I usually eliminate a runner if it has a wins to runs percentage of 5% or less.

A good example of the importance of including consistency in the selection process is provided by the success of a simple system that the American Robert Dowst devised in the 1930s. His approach was based on two factors – class and consistency – and although he developed eleven simple rules for excluding qualifiers the main principle of selection was:

'Bets are limited to horses which have won at least a third of their starts while finishing placed at least half of the time and any qualifying horse has to be the only one of its kind in the race.'

The eleven exclusion rules ensured that the qualifier was not outclassed, that it was running over its correct distance and that it was not too old, lacking in courage or physically infirm. When this simplistic system was first made public it produced excellent profits during both 1936 and 1937, but its success then tailed off as the selections became overplayed. Dowst had argued that 'going public' with his method would have little effect on its profitability, but this proved to be a misjudgement for punters piled into his consistent horses and turned a winning system into a losing one. Nevertheless, the method initially produced an edge and its basic premise, that consistent horses competing within their class can be profitable, should be taken on board.

What Is the Horse's Sex?

Given that this book is about handicap races it may come as a surprise that the sex of a horse should be an issue. After all, horses are handicapped on their ability not on their sex and theoretically the genders should perform equally well in this type of race. In practice, however, they do not and the reason is consistency. The statistics below, which are drawn from two seasons' handicap results, demonstrate that the consistency of a horse is to some extent determined by its sex.

		WINNING RATIOS	
MONTH	**GELDINGS**	**COLTS/HORSES**	**MARES/FILLIES**
MARCH TO APRIL	0.95	1.25	0.82
JUNE TO AUGUST	0.99	1.38	0.65
SEPTEMBER TO NOVEMBER	1.00	1.07	0.93
TOTAL	0.98	1.29	0.75

The table shows that geldings win about the expected number of races and that their performance remains remarkably consistent throughout the season. The fact that they are no longer distracted by the fairer sex is probably the main reason for this! Former trainer Jack Colling once looked after a gelding by the name of High Stakes who raced for nine seasons and from a total of 55 appearances won an incredible 34 races and was placed a further 16 times. Colling was later to remark: 'Give me a stable full of geldings and I'll have the bookmakers crying for mercy.'

Despite their consistency, geldings have a significantly poorer win ratio than colts and entire horses. When I first produced these statistics I was surprised by this finding as I believe that horses normally improve for being gelded. On reflection, I realised that it was logical that the 'entires' should have the upper hand. It is of course the cheap, low-class horses of humble breeding that are commonly gelded because they are unlikely to enjoy a career at stud. Although they generally become more consistent and easier to train as a result of the operation, they tend to be of limited ability.

The more expensive, well-bred horses on the other hand are rarely gelded and they are far more likely to be good than horses with inferior bloodlines. You will not find many gelded horses in the stables of the top trainers and it is the latter who tend to win the majority of the better handicaps with their lightly-raced colts. The statistics show that it pays to give particular attention to the colts, especially during the summer months when they are at their peak, and they usually dominate the big meetings such as Royal Ascot.

As the majority of handicappers aged four or older have been gelded it is worth taking note of any moderately-bred horse that hasn't and asking 'why not'? If the horse is still relatively unexposed it may be a clue that the trainer expects good things from it and believes that it will acquire some stud value in due course.

Fillies and mares are the most inconsistent, particularly during the summer months, and you should be wary of backing one between June and September. Not only do they come in and out of season, but they are also often light-framed and of a slighter build than the other genders. This results in them being less able to stand their racing and they have a tendency to lose their form if subjected to a hard race.

Is the Horse About to Produce its Best Form?

After the field has been narrowed down to its logical contenders the next step is to determine which of the remaining horses are likely to produce their best form in the race. This is the most important stage of the selection process and if you get this right you will make money. The horses still under consideration should all be well drawn, be competing in their class, be suited by the race conditions and be well handicapped. If they produce their best form in the race they will be hard to beat.

However, before backing a horse you must feel sure that it is about to run well. I use the following headings to help me decide this but the list is not exhaustive. For instance you may have read that a horse has been aimed at the race, the owner may be one of the race sponsors, the horse may have won the same race last year, it might usually flourish during this particular month and so on. Again there is always room for intuition and a bit of lateral thinking and you will find that the more time and effort you put into your research the luckier you will become!

RECENT FORM

A horse's recent form is definitely a good guide to how it is likely to perform. A good recent run demonstrates that the horse is fit and well and as long as conditions are favourable it is likely to run with credit again. However, both punters and bookmakers are well aware of this and horses that have either won or placed last time out usually head the market, making it hard to obtain value about them, as the table below shows:

	HORSES THAT FINISHED FIRST, SECOND OR THIRD ON THEIR LAST RUN	HORSES THAT FINISHED NO BETTER THAN TENTH ON THEIR LAST RUN
NUMBER OF WINNERS	344	144
NUMBER OF RUNNERS	2,664	2,336
WINS TO RUNS %	13%	6%
ACCUMULATED WINNING ODDS	1976	1,874
AVERAGE WINNING ODDS	5.7 to 1	13 to 1
TOTAL RETURNS	-£688	-£462

Although the placed horses won just over twice as often than the others, if you had backed every one your pre-tax losses would have been 33% higher than if you had backed all the horses that had finished no better than tenth! Although the results prove that recent form is a good guide when it comes to picking winners, the message is clear: the betting market usually has them covered. For this reason I believe it is better to be patient and wait until you are able to identify a likely, but less obvious contender that is available at decent odds.

There are many valid excuses for a poor run and value can usually be obtained if you are able to identify horses that are in better form than they appear to be to the casual observer. If a horse finished placed on its penultimate run but then ran poorly it is likely to be on offer at around twice the odds it was when it last ran. If there was a valid excuse for the poor run you can safely ignore it and the inflated odds about the horse are likely to be generous.

Excuses for a poor run vary, but typically the horse will have been disadvantaged by the draw or the going, or have been outclassed in its last outing or two. The form of Smart Predator during the 2000 season provides a good example of how this can work in practice. On 1 July, Smart Predator went into my notebook as one to follow when he finished a close second of 19 runners in a race at Newcastle, despite being poorly drawn in stall 11 (draw figure **0.8**). That was a particularly good performance because, despite running out of his class (he carried 8-5 in a 0-95 handicap), he managed to clock a Topspeed rating of 79, which was 7lbs higher than his official rating (72). In view of the fact that he had been disadvantaged by the race conditions he had probably performed better than the bare rating suggested.

On the basis of that run he was sent off the 12-1 fourth favourite in a field of 23 runners at York on 15 July. This ridiculously short price illustrates the betting public's obsession with good recent form, for Smart Predator stood no chance from stall 20 (draw figure **0.4**) and after showing 'good speed' for four furlongs he weakened tamely, recording a Topspeed figure of just 6. On 4 August he ran at Goodwood. On this occasion he had a decent enough draw in stall 12 **(1.0)** but was also dropping in class to a 0-85 handicap and conditions were very much in his favour. However, the public was obviously put off by his poor but excusable showing last time out and he was available at the very generous odds of 25-1. I backed the horse each way to finish in the first four in a 16-runner field and he rewarded my support by finishing third beaten just over a length. Under the circumstances I considered that odds of 5.25 to 1 to finish in the first four represented good value.

As so often happens when a horse is dropped in class Smart Predator posted an improved performance clocking a Topspeed rating of 86. He next ran at Beverley on 16 August and predictably finished unplaced from his coffin draw in stall 1 of 19 **(0.0)**. The public is aware of the bias on the sprint course at Beverley and the horse was sent off at 16-1. His next run was at Yarmouth over 5f on 27 August. He was the second highest rated horse in the race and was well drawn in stall 8 **(1.15)**. The drop back to five from six furlongs looked likely to suit him as he was a front runner and he had recently been leading in the final furlong of six-furlong races before tiring. Furthermore he looked well treated running off a mark of 77 given that he had recently posted a Topspeed rating of 86. He was sent off the 9-2 third favourite in a field of only eight runners and won easily, recording a Topspeed figure of 87 in the process.

It is typical of the betting public that Mizhar and Mousehole were made first and second favourites in the race ahead of Smart Predator despite having no right to be. Mizhar had not won for two years and had performed dismally all season until finishing a close second at Beverley on 16 August in first-time blinkers. He had beaten Smart Predator by eight lengths that day, but had had every right to do so given that he had the best draw of all in stall 19 **(3.0)** compared to Smart Predator's Stall 1 **(0.0)**! On this occasion, however, he was not as well drawn as Smart Predator and on balance the latter's form was clearly superior. Mousehole went off at 11-4 on the strength of a recent win at Sandown despite the fact that this was a 0-90 race and he had only managed to win a race of a higher grade than 0-70 once in 49 attempts! This example demonstrates that to make proper sense of handicap form you have to be able to recognise when a horse has run better or worse than its bare form suggests. You can only do this if you are able to identify the extent to which its past performances were influenced by bias and by its preference or dislike for certain conditions.

Although good recent form is a useful guide to how a horse will perform it is not the key to success most punters think it is. To win money from betting on handicap races you need to acquire a thorough understanding of the numerous reasons why horses perform badly so that you can identify those poor runs that should be excused, and you need to become familiar with the various methods which highlight when a good run is expected by a horse's connections. Avoid the obvious and concentrate on finding reasons why a horse will run better than its odds suggest.

WHAT DO THE HORSE'S ENTRIES INDICATE?

A horse's entries provide valuable clues to whether it will produce its best form. There are no rules that I can give you on this subject because each trainer has his or her own way of operating and you really need to get to know them. Notwithstanding this, it costs the owner money to enter a horse in a race so most trainers refrain from making unnecessary entries. Normally they make a single entry for a horse during a five-day period unless they believe that it is well and ready to produce its best, in which case they may enter the horse in every available suitable race with the intention of finding the easiest opportunity for it. Certain trainers such as Milton (J. M.) Bradley and Mark Johnston regularly have their horses well 'entered up' and it is difficult to read anything into their entries. Experience will teach you which trainers to concentrate on and which ones to ignore.

Perhaps the most profitable period for studying entries is from March to June. Many trainers like to give their horses a few 'quiet' runs at the beginning of the season in order to bring them to full fitness and also in the expectation that their handicap ratings will be lowered. These quiet runs are normally signalled by a single entry and more often than not the horse will be entered to run at a nearby track in order to cut down on travelling costs. In this way it is relatively easy to spot if a trainer believes that a horse is ready and well enough handicapped to win. He will usually signal this by entering the horse for several races within a short period of time, with the intention of finding it the easiest opportunity, and often entries will be made for tracks a long way from the yard. Any sudden increase in the number of entries for a horse should alert you to the likelihood that the trainer thinks it is ready to win.

Whether the horse is good enough or whether it has conditions in its favour come race day are different questions, but when the answers are 'yes' you have found a good bet. If you ignore a horse's poor recent form in these circumstances and trust the trainer's judgement, you will be rewarded with some generously priced winners.

A good example of how this approach can highlight out-of-form horses that are about to run well is provided by Ring Dancer. On 1 June 2001 the gelding ran in a ten-runner sprint handicap at Yarmouth. He had run three times previously during the season and his form figures read -6R8. The fact that he had refused to race on his penultimate start was certainly off-putting but he had performed quite encouragingly on his last run, finishing a fair eighth of 22 runners when not particularly favoured by the conditions of a stakes race at Doncaster. Ring Dancer was trainer-owned by Mrs Linda Stubbs. The entries for trainer-owned horses are especially interesting because the trainers are likely to be particularly circumspect with the number of entries they make, given that they are paying for them!

A look at Ring Dancer's entries before the race showed that on each of his last three runs he had only been entered for the race in which he had competed. However, he had now been entered to run in three races that were all due to take place on the same day! Clearly, Mrs Stubbs felt that her horse was ready to return to form and she was looking to find the most suitable opportunity for him. His official rating had just dropped back to 72, a mark he had won off during the previous season, so she probably also felt that he was well enough handicapped to win. The *Racing Post* offered little encouragement about the horse's chance and out of the ten runners he was ninth in the betting forecast at 16-1. In the event his odds reached a very generous 25-1 and he almost pulled off a satisfying victory for his supporters, but was unfortunately collared close to the line and beaten a neck. This 0-85 handicap was almost certain to provide an opportunity to obtain value because Mousehole was yet again inexplicably made favourite despite his career record of just one win from 49 attempts in races of a class higher than 0-70! The ridiculously short 15-8 market leader predictably finished a never-dangerous seventh.

Other clues can be gleaned from a horse's entries. For example, it is worth paying extra attention to a horse if it runs following a recent withdrawal from another race. On 8 June 2001 at Beverley there were two examples of this type of runner and they illustrate how useful this information can be. The lightly raced three-year-old Madies Pride was entered to run in both the all-aged sprint handicap and the three-year-old sprint handicap which were being run on the same day. She had shown little in four runs since making a fair debut and was officially rated a lowly 48. However, she was unexposed and was something of a dark horse down on bottom weight and her double declaration suggested that her trainer was expecting a good run from her.

Given the importance of a high draw in races over five furlongs at Beverley, John Quinn had presumably employed this strategy in the hope that she would be well drawn in at least one of the two races. He obviously felt that it was worth paying the fixed fine of £420 for making a double declaration. In fact, she had been drawn in stall four of 20 in the all-aged race, but had landed the plum draw of stall 20 in the other. Not surprisingly the news came through later in the day that she had been withdrawn from her first engagement – the all-aged race! The strategy paid off for she won from her pole position at odds of 7-1 having been 12-1 in the *Racing Post's* forecast and after touching 16-1 in a place on course.

The other example involved the mare Mary Jane. The *Racing Post* informed its readers that she had been declared to run the previous afternoon in a better race at Haydock where she would have run from 3lbs out of the handicap had she not been withdrawn by her trainer Nigel Tinkler. A look at the returns for that race showed that unusually 'no reason was given' for her withdrawal. However, it was not unreasonable to conclude that Tinkler had seen the declarations for the Beverley race. On finding that Mary Jane had been allotted the favourable stall 15 in the all-aged sprint, Tinkler probably decided that she would have a better chance at Beverley, where she was also in the handicap proper. It seemed that the trainer was trying to find the best opportunity for his charge and that he was expecting a good run, particularly as the mare was potentially well handicapped on a mark of 45 having previously won when rated 57. In the event Mary Jane ran well, but just failed by a short head to land the rewarding odds of 16-1.

It should be remembered that a trainer will often have a specific race in mind for a horse when planning its campaign. The race in question will often be a valuable handicap, or perhaps a race the horse has won before, or maybe the owner has some connection with it – often in the form of sponsorship. The reason is not important, but when a trainer does have a particular race in mind he is likely to enter the horse for that race only during the relevant five-day period. The horse will be ready and trying but the entries will not provide any clues.

It is useful to compare the number of horses a trainer entered in a particular race at the five day stage with the number of his runners left in come race day. If a trainer enters say five horses in a race, but only leaves one in it at the overnight declaration stage, it suggests that he considers that horse to be the most suitable of his contenders and perhaps he has targeted the race. This is especially relevant when the race is at a track a good distance away from the yard and if the trainer has a good record there. In the chapter *The Theory in Practice* (see page 65) you will see how I used the entries to identify several good bets, particularly a 16-1 winner in the shape of Bodfari Pride.

DID THE HORSE 'LOOK WELL' LAST TIME OUT?

A horse's appearance is a good guide to its fitness and general well-being. If you are by the paddock before a race and observe a horse with a gleaming coat and plenty of muscle definition in the neck and legs, with no signs of flab, you can be pretty confident that the horse is fit and ready to run well if conditions are favourable. *Raceform* make reference to the appearance of horses in their invaluable paddock comments and they describe horses fitting the above profile as having 'looked well'.

The importance of a horse appearing to be fit and well, particularly in the first few months of a season, cannot be overstated, as the following table demonstrates. It shows the wins to runs percentage of those horses described by *Raceform* as having 'looked well' and the wins to runs percentage of those that did not attract the comment from March to May.

| RACEFORM | WINS TO RUNS PERCENTAGES | |
PADDOCK COMMENT	MARCH & APRIL	MAY
'LOOKED WELL'	14.2 %	13.1 %
OTHER	5.6 %	6.9 %

The effect is more pronounced at the beginning of the season when fitness is at a premium and there are fewer horses that attract the comment. In the season I analysed horses described as having "looked well' between March and May accounted for only 22% of the total number of runners but won 38% of the races – an excellent winning ratio of **1.7**.

Of course in order to benefit fully from this information you have to attend the meetings so that you can see the horses in the paddock before they run. However, it is still possible to put the information to good use. To do this you need to purchase *Raceform's* Official Form Book, or the weekly *Raceform Update*, because to my knowledge they are the only organisation that publish paddock comments. Most handicappers take a few runs to come to hand at the start of the season and do not attract the 'looked well' comment until their third or fourth run at least. Look out for the occasion when a horse first attracts the comment during a season. You will have missed the boat if the horse either won or ran well, but if it did not, look to see if there was a valid excuse such as a bad draw. As long as the horse is running again within two weeks it will probably still be at peak fitness. If the trainer has placed it to best advantage (the number of entries may provide a clue in this respect) and conditions are now favourable it is likely to run well at generous odds given its moderate-looking early season form.

There are other *Raceform* paddock comments that are well worth noting. Occasionally a three- or four-year-old will attract the comment 'Has Done Well' (h.d.w) on its first run of the season. A horse that attracts the comment has matured physically during the winter months and has made up into a fine-looking animal. There is a good chance that the horse will show improved form once it reaches peak fitness and it pays to monitor their progress closely.

Another informative comment is 'backward'. Horses that attract this comment are considered to be well short of peak fitness and usually need a few runs before coming to hand. Again it pays to follow their progress and to keep an eye on the entries to see when the trainer attempts to place them to win. By the time they reach peak fitness their ratings will usually have been lowered by the Handicapper and they may be well treated.

Raceform also inform you if a horse wore leg bandages when it ran. Front leg bandages in particular are a negative sign and usually indicate that the horse has sustained an injury, particularly if they are being worn following a lengthy absence from the track. Horses wearing front leg bandages should be treated with caution, particularly when the ground is riding fast.

WHAT FORM IS THE TRAINER IN?

Assessing whether a trainer is out of form is easy because the *Racing Post* provides a comprehensive daily guide that shows how many days have elapsed since each trainer last saddled a winner. There are all sorts of reasons why trainers' horses run below form for lengthy periods but the most common are viral infections. Other reasons can be more obscure. I remember when a certain yard hardly had a winner one year and the trainer blamed his poor form on the fact that a nearby farmer had decided to grow oilseed rape. The pollen from this notorious plant had caused a severe allergic reaction among his horses! Whatever the reason the result is the same: the affected yard's horses run below form.

I think it is a mistake to automatically eliminate the runners from out-of-form yards because you can miss some good priced winners as a result. However, if a medium or large-sized yard has not had a winner in the last 14 days, or its wins to runners strike rate is well below normal, you do not want to take a short price about one of their runners! I do not pay any attention to the poor form of small yards because they rarely have any winners anyway.

The trainer statistics also highlight those handlers that are in good form. If a trainer has had a winner within the last day or two and has a wins to runners strike rate during the last 14 days that is considerably higher than his or her seasonal average, his or her runners should be closely watched. They are more than likely to produce their best form if conditions are favourable. This is definitely a positive factor.

Watch out for trainers who have been hopelessly out of form for a long period of time – usually a couple of months or more – and take note when they finally register a handicap winner. This is the best indicator of a revival in the fortunes of a yard. As soon as things do improve the stable's runners will merit particular attention. Its handicappers will usually have run several times at least without success during the lean spell and their ratings will have dropped as a result. By the time the stable returns to form its handicappers tend to be well treated and ready to win races when conditions suit. For this reason yards returning to form after a long spell in the doldrums often rattle off winners in a short space of time and the odds on offer about their horses can be generous in view of their recent poor form.

IS THE HORSE'S STYLE OF RUNNING SUITED BY THE TRACK?

The majority of tracks tend to favour either horses that race prominently or those that are held up for a late run. If you understand how the bias works at each course you can use this knowledge not only to explain a poor run but also to anticipate a return to form. A good example of this in practice was provided by Indian Bazaar at Lingfield on 24 June 2001.

This gelding had won two successive races when making all the running over five furlongs at Goodwood and Yarmouth two tracks that slightly favour front runners over sprint distances, both with win ratios of **1.4**. He then ran at Bath in a higher-class race and carried 2lbs overweight. Once again he attempted to make all, but finished fourth of 12 runners, just over three lengths behind the winner. The first three horses were all favoured by being held up for a late run. His performance was better than it probably appeared to the casual observer because not only was he outclassed and carrying overweight, but his style of running was unsuited to Bath which has the biggest bias in favour of held-up horses in the country. The win ratio of horses that lead or race prominently on Bath's sprint course is a dismal **0.8**; under the circumstances Indian Bazaar ran with a lot of credit. His next run was at Lingfield on 24 June. He had been dropped in class from a 0-85 to a 0-70 handicap and was 2lbs better off in the ratings because he was no longer carrying overweight. He also had a fair draw in stall nine. The most significant factor, however, was that Lingfield favoured his style of running (the win ratio of prominent horses is **1.7**); it was indeed more suitable than Goodwood and Yarmouth had been! These factors suggested that the gelding was likely to find things a lot easier than when he ran at Bath and there was every chance that he would return to winning ways. He went on to win at 11-2 and raced prominently throughout.

OTHER THINGS TO CONSIDER

There are so many things that can be taken into consideration that it is impractical to provide a comprehensive list here. It really depends on how much work you are prepared to put in and how thorough your approach is. For example, there is a lot of useful information that can be gleaned from reading the *Racing Post* on a daily basis, particularly the results section, as well as *Raceform Update* and the *Weekender*. You can find out about injuries, operations that horses have had, future targets and the trainer's thoughts about a horse's going and distance preferences. If you make a note of this information it can be used later to give you a valuable insight into whether a horse is about to run well or not.

A good example of this is provided by the record of To the Roof. Before the 1996 season, To The Roof had run eight times without success and on his first appearance as a four-year-old he ran off the moderate rating of 67. There was no obvious reason to believe that the horse was well handicapped. But after he won his second start of the campaign by three lengths I made a note of his trainer Peter Harris' revelation that the horse had had a tie-back operation to improve his breathing during the close season, and I had discovered that the horse had also been gelded. Both operations can bring about marked improvement; To The Roof's convincing victory suggested strongly that he was better for them and that he was one to follow. He rewarded his supporters by winning three of his next four starts at odds of 100-30, 10-1 and 6-1, and by the end of the season his official rating had risen to 99. In fact it was subsequently to become 45lbs higher than the rating he had at the time he went under the knife, and this demonstrates the effect that operations can have.

Both the trainer's and the horse's record at the course are worth noting and can be either a positive or a negative factor. The distance a horse has travelled to the track is of interest too whilst jockey bookings also provide clues. I have for instance found several good winners in the past after spotting that a particular jockey has mounts booked at two courses during the same afternoon. I can remember successfully backing Sailormaite at 12-1 in the opening race at a Haydock meeting after noting that Dean McKeown had decided to go there just for that ride prior to travelling to Doncaster to take part in the last few races. Jockey comradeship can also have an influence on the outcome of a race. It is surely no coincidence that most of the top riders seem to win on their first mount after returning from a long absence. I wonder how many jockeys, with the exception of Pat Eddery, were really trying to prevent Frankie Dettori landing the last leg of his 'Magnificent Seven' at Ascot. In the chapter *The Theory in Practice* (see page 65) I mention some other factors that I occasionally take into consideration.

As I have said potential sources of useful information are almost limitless but it is often hard to know the worth of most of it until after the race! With experience you get to know what is important and you will probably give the most credence to what has worked for you in the past.

CHAPTER SIX

DECIDING WHEN AND WHEN NOT TO BET

When you have gone to the trouble of analysing a race in detail there can be an over-riding desire to place a bet. This may be even though you have been unable to find a selection that either fully meets the requirements of your method or, nevertheless, gives you a gut feeling that it is going to run well. You must acquire the mental discipline to overcome such urges otherwise you will face a lot of self-recrimination when things inevitably go wrong. Be patient and wait for another day. As *Timeform*'s Phil Bull once said: 'You cannot construct good bets, you have to wait for them to come along.' My method usually narrows a race down to three or four contenders and it is necessary to choose between them. If there are more than four contenders I leave the race alone on the grounds that it is too competitive. I do, however, make an exception for the season's major handicaps.

The contenders fit the same profile in that they are well drawn and well handicapped, they are running in their correct class, they are suited by the prevailing conditions and are hopefully about to produce their best form. Because they have the same basic things in their favour they usually have a broadly similar chance of either winning or placing and in my experience their position in the betting market does not have a significant bearing on the likelihood of them winning. In fact, last season the average odds of the selections I made were 13-1, but interestingly the average odds of those that won were higher at 14-1. I suspect that this was a statistical blip, but nevertheless, it suggests that the price of a contender has only a marginal bearing on its chance.

Because the contenders fit a similar profile the most important consideration when choosing between them has to be their odds; preference should usually be given to the contender with the longest price. However, there are other considerations. Which of the contenders has the best draw figure, which is the classiest, which is the best hand-icapped and which of them is the most likely to produce its best form? It is basically a question of balancing these considerations against the available odds and making a decision. I can not teach you this, but with experience you will probably make the right decision more often than not. Last season I made the right choice between the contenders about 60% of the time, but there were, of course, plenty of occasions when the winner was not one of the contenders!

Once you have decided which horse or horses to back you have to decide what bets to place. I choose to back each way when I obtain odds of 12-1 or more, even though I know that each-way betting theoretically reduces my profits in the long-term. To maximise profits it is better to put the place element of the wager on as a win bet and wait for a winner. Although there will be more losing bets the winning ones will invariably produce a bigger profit than the total returns from the split stakes on the each-way bets. Having checked my results from last season, I know that I would have made far more money if I had bet my total stake win only. However, although it sounds perverse I will continue to bet each way because I do not respond well to long losing runs, which affect my confidence.

It sounds rather weak I know, but I prefer to accept reduced profits in exchange for the security of each-way betting, because the occasional long losing run is inevitable when you regularly bet on outsiders. Last season, for example, if I had bet win only, my longest losing run would have been eleven, but because I bet each way the longest sequence I had to endure was only five and that was relatively easy to cope with! I placed 22 each-way bets and the average odds about the selections was nearly 20-1. Eleven of them placed and returned a profit of 41 points to level stakes. Of course, if I had split my usual stake in half to cover each part of the bet I would have made a profit of 20.5 points. But I believe if you bet each way it is better to treat it as two bets and place your usual stake on both the win and the place portions.

THE NEED FOR VALUE

Before making a selection, the question of whether it represents value also needs to be addressed. This is certainly a controversial subject for although the basic premise that you will only win in the long-term if you regularly accept odds larger than your selection's true chance of winning is undeniably true, there is no magic formula for *accurately* assessing a horse's true chance of winning! Of course it is possible to make an educated guess and both the betting forecasters and the bookmakers do exactly that every day. However, although they can make an educated guess as to a horse's winning chance, it remains just that. As followers of Pricewise in the *Racing Post* will acknowledge, the forecasters' guesswork often proves to be hopelessly inaccurate!

For this reason I would caution against attempting to produce your own odds. For the figures to be in any way trustworthy it is necessary to devote most of the morning to producing them and if you adopt a more simplistic method that is quicker to use, the accuracy of the odds is likely to be woeful. Okay, perhaps they can provide a useful guide, but if you are looking for a decent assessment of each horse's winning chance why not just take Ladbrokes' early prices and strip out their profit margin?

Assessing value boils down to differences in opinion your opinion against those of other punters and layers. Whether or not your opinion is right frequently enough is best judged on the evidence of a season's betting. If by the end of the season you have made a level-stakes profit you have obtained value, but if, despite knowing one end of the *Racing Post* from the other, you have made a loss, your methods are probably too similar to most other punters and your edge is blunt!

In order to get an idea of what odds are likely to represent value, you need to establish what the winning strike-rates are of the particular methods you employ and how the strike-rates are affected by the odds of your selections and the number of runners in a race. Only then can you draw any conclusions about the sort of prices you need to obtain in order to show a profit in the long-term.

My records from the last couple of seasons show that the average number of runners in the races that I bet on was 17 and that about one in five of my selections won. This means that after building in a profit margin and taking tax into account, there is little point in me backing horses below 6-1. Of course 6-1 is only an average and the price I am actually prepared to accept about a selection depends on the number of runners in the race. I use the factor of 2.8 (17 divided by 6) to determine the odds that are acceptable in relation to the number of runners. If there are 30 runners the minimum price that I am prepared to accept is 11-1 (30 divided by 2.8) and in a six-runner race the minimum acceptable price would be 9-4. Although this certainly does not give an accurate reflection of every selection's winning chance, I believe that it provides me with a useful guide to the prices I need to obtain to show a profit in the long-term. No doubt on occasions I take odds about a horse that are too short in relation to its true chance of winning, but I am confident that over the course of a season I will obtain sufficient value about other selections to more than compensate for the inevitable errors that I make.

THE IMPORTANCE OF KEEPING RECORDS

The only way to determine the odds you need to obtain in order to realise a profit in the long-term is by referring to your past betting records. If you are intending to take your betting seriously it is imperative that you keep proper records of all your bets, if for no other reason than to establish whether you are winning or losing! Whenever I analyse a race I make comprehensive notes explaining the thinking behind the decisions I take. I complete one of the forms shown below to ensure that I approach each race in a structured way and that I give proper consideration to all of the factors that I believe to be important. I admit that filling in the form can be a bit of a pain at times. On occasions I have to force myself to do it, particularly when I feel that I have identified a good selection from an initial perusal of the paper, or when a horse is running that I have been waiting to back. However, it is important to be disciplined and to give every horse due consideration, otherwise it is all too easy to overlook something that will appear irritatingly obvious with the benefit of hindsight! Furthermore, reading over the forms at a later date is a useful way to identify your strengths and weaknesses; I know that they have helped me to improve my ability to make the right choice between the contenders.

An example of a race assessment form that I completed during the 2000 season is shown on page 66. If you own a computer you will be able to produce something similar on it and I strongly recommend that you do. The form that I use has five boxes alongside the name of each contender.

Perhaps I should explain what the figures in the boxes mean. The **TRAINER** box contains two numbers. The first is the trainer's wins to runs percentage over the last 14 days and the figure in brackets is the number of days since the yard's last winner. The figure in the **RATING** box shows how well handicapped the horse is and is produced by taking the average of its best two Topspeed ratings, deducting seven and then comparing the resultant figure to the horse's official rating. The **DRAW** box shows the horse's individual draw figure (if a bias exists). The **PACE** box simply records each horse's pace figure so that its probable early position in the race can be determined, and the figure in the **W/R** box is the horse's wins to runs percentage.

COURSE: EPSOM   GOING: GOOD TO SOFT   DATE: 10.06.00

STALL	20	19	18	17	16	15	14	13	12	11	10	9	8	7	6	5	4	3	2	1
				3	0	2	2	0	0	2	8	4	0	7	2	13	0	2	10	0

PACE COMMENT — *THREE PROBABLE FRONT RUNNERS SO A STRONG PACE LOOKS GUARANTEED. THE PACE IS CONCENTRATED ON THE INSIDE OF THE COURSE. THIS TRACK STRONGLY FAVOURS HORSES THAT RACE PROMINENTLY BUT GIVEN THE LIKELY STRONG PACE THOSE THAT CHASE THE LEADERS MAY DO BEST.*

DRAW COMMENT — *NO REAL ADVANTAGE AT THIS DISTANCE PARTICULARLY WHEN THE GROUND IS RIDING ON THE SOFT SIDE.*

DRAW ELIMINATIONS NONE

	HORSE	OTHER ELIMINATIONS
1	SURVEYOR	FIRST TIME OUT. NOT WON SINCE 1997
2	RUSSIAN BOY	3YO. NOT WELL-HANDICAPPED
3	SILCA BLANKA, DEBBIE'S WARNING, NOMORE MR NICEGUY, ELMHURST BOY	ALL NEED FURTHER THAN A DOWNHILL SIX FURLONGS
4	JUWWI	NEEDS FASTER GROUND AND TRAINER OUT OF FORM
5	THE FUGATIVE	EXCELLENT RECORD AT EPSOM BUT POORLY HANDICAPPED NOW (-7)
6	FIRST MAITE	PREFERS SOFTER GROUND AND A MORE GALLOPING TRACK
7	ALISTAIR SMELLIE, DELEGATE, WAX LYRICAL	ALL OUT OF FORM AND NOTHING TO SUGGEST IMPROVEMENT

CONTENDERS	TRAINER	RATING	DRAW	PACE	W/R%
FURTHER OUTLOOK	10(4)	+5	N/A	8	16

WON THIS RACE LAST YEAR OFF A 7LBS LOWER MARK BUT DID GO ON TO WIN OFF TODAY'S RATING SO HE LOOKS FAIRLY TREATED. CAME BACK TO FORM LAST TIME OUT ON HIS SIXTH RUN OF THE SEASON SO NO SURPRISE IF HE HAS BEEN TRAINED WITH THIS VALUABLE PRIZE IN MIND. HAS A FAVOURITE'S CHANCE BUT WILL NOT HAVE EVERYTHING HIS OWN WAY UPFRONT AGAINST TWO OTHER FRONT RUNNERS.

	TRAINER	RATING	DRAW	PACE	W/R%
ROYAL RESULT	10 (4)	+4	N/A	2	13

NOT SHOWN MUCH THIS SEASON BUT HAS NOT HAD GROUND CONDITIONS TO SUIT. HE HAS AN EXCELLENT RECORD WHEN THERE IS GIVE IN THE GROUND AND HE HAS THAT TODAY. LOOKS FAIRLY TREATED AT PRESENT AND WILL BENEFIT FROM A. NICHOLLS' 3LBS CLAIM. WILL ALSO LIKE THE STRONG PACE THAT IS SURE TO BE SET TODAY BUT GIVEN HIS FINE RECORD IN THE BIG HANDICAPS I SUSPECT THAT A STIFFER TRACK AND A BIGGER FIELD OF RUNNERS WOULD BE IDEAL.

	TRAINER	RATING	DRAW	PACE	W/R%
GET STUCK IN	5 (5)	+3	N/A	13	10

HAS EXCELLENT SPEED AND WILL DOUBTLESS LEAD THE FIELD HERE. THIS SHARP TRACK AND SOFT GOING ARE LIKELY TO BE IDEAL. LOOKS FAIRLY TREATED AND HE RAN WELL TWO RUNS AGO WHEN A CLOSE SIXTH OF 28 RUNNERS AT NEWMARKET. WAS UNSUITED BY THE CONDITIONS AND THE DRAW LAST TIME OUT SO MAY WELL BOUNCE BACK TO FORM HERE. THE HORSE HAS TRAVELLED OVER 400 MILES DOWN TO EPSOM FOR THIS PRIZE AND IS OBVIOUSLY HERE TO WIN. IT IS UNFORTUNATE THAT TWO OTHER FRONT RUNNERS ARE IN THE RACE BUT HE HAS SO MUCH EARLY SPEED THAT THEY MAY STRUGGLE TO GET NEAR HIM AND HE MAY HOLD ON.

	TRAINER	RATING	DRAW	PACE	W/R%
FIRE DOME	10 (2)	+8	N/A	2	21

LOOKS PARTICULARLY WELL-HANDICAPPED AT PRESENT. PRIOR TO READILY WINNING HIS FIRST HANDICAP LAST TIME OUT HE HAD WON TWO CLAIMERS IN A ROW BUT WAS DROPPED 4LBS IN THE OFFICIAL RATINGS. HE WAS RATED 105 LAST SEASON AND RUNS OFF ONLY 80 TODAY AND COULD POTENTIALLY BE THROWN IN NOW THAT HE HAS RETURNED TO FORM. HE HAS AN EXCELLENT WIN RATIO AND LOVES GOOD/SOFT GROUND ON WHICH HE HAS WON FIVE RACES FROM ONLY NINE STARTS! HIS RECENT WIN CAME AT LINGFIELD WHICH SUGGESTS THAT HE WILL HANDLE THIS DOWNHILL TRACK. MUST HAVE A GREAT CHANCE AT A GOOD PRICE.

CONCLUSION   *QUITE HARD TO CHOOSE BETWEEN THE MAIN CONTENDERS BUT AS ROYAL RESULT IS YET TO STRIKE FORM AND PREFERS A STIFFER TRACK I WILL PASS ON HIM. FURTHER OUTLOOK HAS TO BE RESPECTED BUT AT THE FORECAST PRICES HE MAKES LESS APPEAL THAN THE OTHER TWO GIVEN THAT HE WILL NOT BE ABLE TO DOMINATE FROM THE FRONT AS HE LIKES TO DO. FIRE DOME AND GET STUCK IN BOTH APPEAL AT BIG PRICES AND I WOULD NOT WANT TO PICK ONE AT THE EXPENSE OF THE OTHER.*

SELECTION	FIRE DOME (12-1 TAKEN)	WIN £	PLACE £
FORECASTS	FIRE DOME, FURTHER OUTLOOK & GET STUCK IN	6 X £	= £
OTHER BETS	GET STUCK IN (14-1 TAKEN)	£	

RESULT

1ST	FIRE DOME 11-1
2ND	FURTHER OUTLOOK 11-2
3RD	ROYAL RESULT 16-1
4TH	DELEGATE 8-1
5TH	GET STUCK IN 10-1
DISTANCE:	$1^3/_4$, $^1/_2$, $2^1/_2$, $1^1/_4$

RUNNING TOTAL   £   **POINTS TOTAL**

You will notice in the example that I backed two horses in the same race. I see nothing wrong with increasing one's chance of winning, as long as the available odds are big enough to compensate for the additional bet, or bets made. In this case I fancied Get Stuck In and Fire Dome and I was happy to back both because I considered that they were both available at value odds. There were 16 runners and thus the minimum price I would usually be prepared to accept was 6-1 (16 divided by 2.8), but in this example the minimum needed to be increased to 7-1 to compensate for the inevitable one point loss sustained from the loser. As Get Stuck In was 14-1 and Fire Dome available at 12-1. I was confident that they both represented good value.

CHAPTER SEVEN

THE THEORY IN PRACTICE

This chapter details some of the selections I made during the 2000 season. There is insufficient space to provide you with the complete list so I have chosen those I think offer the best insight into my methods. The majority of the selections I have included here either successfully landed a win or an each-way bet. I have chosen them not in an effort to inflate my ego, but because they are obviously the best examples I have of my method in practice. I have included some losing bets that I feel are, nevertheless, instructive. Of course during the season I backed considerably more losers than winners, but as the minimum price I took was 13-2 that is no surprise.

SUNLEY SENSE
10-1   *11 June 2000, Chester, 5F*

This was the first selection I made during the 2000 season, after having as usual sat out the first month or so of the campaign. I began by eliminating the six runners that had negative draws (stalls 7-12). Of the remaining six, Sunley Sense caught my eye. In an interview with the *Racing Post* at the beginning of the season, trainer Mick Channon had given Sunley Sense a very favourable mention and I had made a note to remind me to keep an eye on him. Channon was of the opinion that following a gelding operation during the winter Sunley Sense had improved and was sure to win races.

Sunley Sense had been unplaced on his first two runs of the season but performed with credit last time when eighth of 24 from a poor draw (0.6) at Thirsk, finishing only one and a half lengths behind Ziggy's Dancer who was first of the far-side group. Despite having run well the horse had been dropped a further 3lbs by the Handicapper, and was clearly potentially well handicapped if the gelding operation could bring about a return to his old form. He started the 1999 season on a rating of 99 (16lbs higher than his new mark). Although he was set to carry only 8-5 in weight he was not outclassed. This was a 'Rated' handicap in which the weights are depressed by 7lbs – in a normal handicap Sunley Sense would have carried 8-12 – and he had shown himself to be of a higher class in the past. Given that he was likely to be at peak fitness following two runs and that he was now well drawn (1.6) I considered that he was excellent value at 10-1 and I backed him each way as I felt sure that he would at least place. He finished second but was always going to be beaten by Damalis who did well to win from stall 6 and went on to better things later in the season.

SHIRLEY NOT

13-2   *13 May 2000, Beverley, 5F*

I began by eliminating all the horses with negative draws. Out of the 20 runners only five had positive draws so the remaining 15 were given the chop! I then eliminated Palvic Lady and Bodfari Komaite who were having their first runs of the season. They usually need a couple of runs before hitting form and also the latter appeared to be Mick Easterby's second 'string' behind William's Well. This nearly proved to be a costly error because I had forgotten that Bodfari Komaite had in fact already 'run', having completed the course at Newcastle on 24 April after ducking under the stalls.

Shirley Not had the best draw in stall 20 and had a significantly better draw figure (2.4) than the remaining two contenders which had figures of 1.5 and 1.2. Furthermore, he was carrying 9-10 and was thus one of the class horses in the race. This was the gelding's third run of the season so he was likely to be fully fit. He had been 'backward' first time out and had performed poorly, but the second time he ran he finished a good third of 13 behind the improving Indian Spark and was subsequently dropped a generous-looking 2lbs by the Handicapper. His previous Topspeed figures suggested that he was well treated and this fact coupled with his plum draw was sure to make him a very hard horse to beat, particularly as he was in good form. The fact that he usually raced 'in touch' with the leaders meant that he was likely to be ideally placed in the early stages of the race (horses in the 'chased leaders' group do best in these races). He was also likely to make full use of his draw rather than surrendering his advantage as a result of being held up at the back of the field. I backed him to win at 13-2. In the event he just scraped home from Bodfari Komaite (draw figure 2.4) who was heavily gambled on from a forecast 20-1 into 5-1 and whose supporters were unlucky not to collect. The well-drawn pair finished three lengths clear of the remainder. Shirley Not was subsequently raised a stiff-looking 7lbs for the win, which was not justified, given how favoured he had been by the draw. Not surprisingly he went on to struggle off his new rating and the draw factor should have alerted punters to avoid him.

NORTHERN SVENGALI

25-1   *19 May 2000, Thirsk, 5F*

Only the horses in the highest five stalls had positive draws so the remaining 18 were eliminated. Northern Svengali had performed with credit earlier in the season when fourth of 16 in a seven-furlong handicap at Catterick, despite not getting the best of runs. Since then he had been unplaced three times, but on two occasions the ground had been unsuitably soft and last time out in a seven-furlong race at Thirsk the ground had been no firmer than good. I felt sure that he was a sprinter, not a seven-furlong horse, and that the key to him was fast ground (on good to firm ground his record was 1st, 2nd and 4th).

He had a favourable draw (1.12), was dropping in class into a 0-75 handicap for the first time that season, had his ideal conditions of six furlongs on fast ground and he was well handicapped having been dropped 7lbs since his Catterick fourth. Furthermore, he was reasonably consistent for a sprinter having been placed 11 times from 26 runs. He looked excellent each-way value at 25-1 and I bet accordingly. In the event he disappointed and was never in the race. With the benefit of hindsight, perhaps I should have been more worried by his poor showing last time out at Thirsk on good ground. I should also have been concerned by the fact that he was unlikely to have the speed to race prominently. However, I still feel that his price of 25-1 was big enough to compensate for these doubts.

INDIAN SPARK

25-1   *27 May 2000, Haydock, 5F*

During the 1999 season I noticed that low to middle numbered stalls seemed to have the edge at Haydock, particularly when the ground was on the soft side, whereas in the past the high numbers had been favoured. This realisation had led me to back a good winner in the shape of Ivory's Joy at 20-1 on 25 September (drawn 2 of 20) and I was keen to get stuck into the low numbers again in 2000.

I began by eliminating the runners in stalls 21-11 that included the first eight in the betting forecast! If I was right the race had an ideal shape to it and I was bound to obtain value about my selection! Of those drawn low, Indian Spark simply stood out. I had noticed that, unusually for a six-year-old, he had been gelded during the winter, and there was evidence to suggest that it may have done him good. He had surprisingly been made favourite on his second run of the season when terribly drawn at Thirsk in stall 2 of 11 (0.5) on soft ground. He had done well to finish fourth behind the runners in stalls 9, 7 and 11. Considering that he had done nothing special first time out and that the crowd at Thirsk are pretty conscious of the draw, the gamble hinted that the stable, or somebody else, was expecting good things from the horse.

This suspicion was confirmed when he was very heavily backed on his next run when well drawn at Newcastle on soft ground (3-1 into 13-8 fav) and he won easily by three lengths. He recorded a Topspeed figure of 93 which was far higher than his official rating of 78 and suggested that the horse was potentially well handicapped. Given that he had won a 0-100 handicap in 1997 when rated 98, the Topspeed figure looked credible, particularly as the gelding operation may have brought about a revival. Furthermore, the form was subsequently franked by Shirley Not's win at Beverley.

On his next outing Indian Spark ran with credit at Hamilton, finishing fifth of 18 on unsuitably fast ground, and followed that by finishing 20th of 23 at York. This dismal showing was excusable, however, because he had been poorly drawn in stall 16, his jockey had kept him towards the unfavoured stands side and the ground had been too firm. Nevertheless it ensured that his price would be generous next time! The horse was now well drawn in stall six and had his ideal conditions of five furlongs and soft ground and I was sure that he was still well handicapped despite the fact that his rating had been raised to 85. Furthermore, the pace figures suggested that he would have the advantage of racing prominently in the early stages. I was amazed to see that Hills were offering 25-1 about him and I backed the horse each way. In the event Indian Spark won nicely and he was later to do me another good turn when going on to win a Listed race when drawn in stall 1 at Chester, confirming the apparent improvement brought about by the gelding operation.

BODFARI PRIDE

16-1   *1 June 2000, Goodwood, 6F*

Of all the bets I placed during the 2000 season this one gave me the most satisfaction. On the face of it Bodfari Pride had no chance. Having missed the 1999 season through injury he appeared to have deteriorated on the evidence of his first three runs for his new trainer David Nicholls, having been beaten 16 lengths, 22 lengths and 27 lengths. The *Racing Post's* Spotlight assessment was: 'Little cause for optimism in recent starts and hard to fancy'. The horse was forecast to be the 16-1 outsider.

However, there were good reasons to believe that he was about to run a big race. Nicholls' horses usually need a few runs at the beginning of the season before they reach full fitness and one of the benefits of this is that they drop a few pounds in the official ratings. Bodfari Pride had started the season on a mark of 73 and had dropped down to 64, making him potentially well handicapped given that he had previously won a handicap when rated 73. On his first two runs of the season he had been ridden by a 7lbs claimer and showed little. On his penultimate run over seven furlongs at Chester, Franny Norton had taken over but on that occasion the horse had a poor draw in stall 15 (0.4). Despite being beaten by 27 lengths he showed some promise by displaying good speed to remain prominent until a quarter of a mile out when his wide draw took its toll and he weakened.

The horse was now set to run at Goodwood where Nicholls had an excellent record, scoring with 9 of his 47 runners (19%). He was the only horse the stable had sent on the 546-mile round trip and the fact that Norton had also travelled down to take the ride suggested a good run was expected. Furthermore, a look at the entries showed that Nicholls had entered three horses for the race but had obviously decided to rely on Bodfari Pride. The clincher was that when I looked back at the horse's past entries I noted that he had only been entered for the one race each time he had run so far this season, but this week his trainer had entered him for three races. This strongly suggested that the horse was now in peak condition and ready to strike. The draw was of no significance in a field of only ten runners so his number five stall was not a problem and he had already proven that he was well suited by soft ground.

David Nicholls normally converts his runners to sprinters irrespective of their past form so the fact that the horse had only won over seven furlongs in the past was not a problem either. In view of the above I felt confident that Bodfari Pride was going to run a big race and that 16-1 represented excellent value. I backed the horse each way. In the event it was a close-run thing but he managed to make all and held on by a rapidly diminishing head.

TORRENT

7-1   *5 June 2000, Thirsk, 5F*

When I saw the betting forecast for this race I was very keen to get involved as it had the ideal 'shape' to it. The first two in the betting had to be opposed and if I could find a selection I was virtually guaranteed to obtain a value price. The forecast favourite William's Well had a coffin draw (0.5) and was certain to struggle. The second favourite Shirley Not was, as I have already mentioned, on my list of horses to oppose after he had been raised a harsh 7lbs following his short-head win at Beverley when he was decisively advantaged by the draw.

Of the well-drawn horses, Torrent in stall nine (1.45) caught my eye. I liked Torrent because he seemed very well handicapped on his best form from the previous season. He was also dropping in class slightly following a good run last time when he finished three lengths behind some in-form horses, despite having been slowly into stride. He had been apprentice ridden on all his three runs so far this season but George Duffield had been booked to ride (a positive sign) and he had run well in the past on soft ground. My doubt was that Torrent was wearing blinkers (as he had done for quite some time) because I had noticed that he had recorded easily his best Topspeed figures when running without the headgear. Although he had been running consistently with them on he had not been finding much in a finish. Despite this doubt I thought that he was still value at 7-1 and backed him to win. In the event he finished a rather disappointing fourth, once again finding 'no extra' in the final stages. Victory went to the well-drawn Mukarrab from stall eight (1.12) at 12-1. As anticipated the well-backed favourite Shirley Not disappointed his followers by finishing a poor eighth, but William's Well hinted at better things to come by coming an excellent third from his poor draw.

BOLD EFFORT

10-1   *13 June 2000, Salisbury, 6F*

The high numbers have the advantage on fast ground at Salisbury. Given that the only front runner in the race was drawn high I was confident that the high numbers would dominate, so I began by eliminating stalls 1-10. Of those drawn high two were three-year-olds, two needed softer ground and one was totally out of form so they were eliminated, which left only four contenders. Of these, Bold Effort looked to be overpriced at 10-1. He was in form and potentially very well handicapped with an official rating of 76, given that earlier in his career he had won a handicap off 92. This impression was confirmed by his excellent run last time out when, despite being impeded at the start, he came with a strong run to finish second of 16 at Newbury. What distinguished that as a good performance was that he recorded a Topspeed figure of 90 that suggested that the horse was still well treated, even though the Handicapper had responded by raising his rating from 73 to 76.

Bold Effort was ideally suited by an uphill track and had previously won at the course. The fast ground was not a problem and he was drawn 18 of 19 so the conditions of the race were very much in his favour. The one doubt was that he was usually held up in his races and there was a danger that he might struggle to obtain a clear run in the closing stages if the field bunched towards the far side as normal. However, I felt that his price of 10-1 more than compensated for that possibility and I was also pleased to see that Richard Hughes had been booked for the ride as he is particularly adept at riding a waiting race. In the event Bold Effort failed to obtain a clear run and was switched to the centre two furlongs out, but fortunately he still managed to come with a strong late run to win 'readily'.

STORYTELLER

20-1   16 June 2000, York, 5F

The low numbers have the advantage at York and most of the runners with early pace were drawn low so I began by eliminating stalls 11-22. Of the remainder, one was blinkered for the first time, two were outclassed, one needed softer ground and two were having their first outing of the season and would need the run so they were all eliminated. This left four contenders and of those I favoured Storyteller as he looked overpriced at 20-1. He was well drawn in stall 2 and his rating of 78 meant he was well handi-capped. Not only had he won off a mark of 80 the previous season, but he had also recorded a Topspeed figure of 85 when coming third at Thirsk a few runs earlier.

Having checked Storyteller's entries I was sure that his trainer meant to win with him. He had run four times already and each time he had run he had only been entered for the race he competed in. This time, however, the horse had been entered for three races due to take place over the weekend and it was clear that Michael Dods was trying to find the best opportunity for the horse. This conclusion was supported by the fact that the horse had won on his fifth run of the previous season and I felt that the trainer was trying to repeat the trick on this occasion. The horse also had an excellent wins to runs rate of 21% and was obviously a trier. With conditions in his favour and with the entries indicating that today was the day I was very confident of a big run, although I would have been happier if it had been a stiffer five furlongs which would have suited the horse better. I backed him each way at 20-1. In the event he finished third, less than a length behind the horses drawn in stalls 5 and 4 and kept on well in the final furlong.

ICE

16-1   17 June 2000, York, 9F

I began by eliminating the runners in stalls 5-16 which all had negative draws! Of the remaining four, Ice looked to be an excellent bet. He had an overall winning strike rate of 32% that is very high for a handicapper that has run 19 times, and he had won three out of three at York, demonstrating an obvious liking for the course. Usually ridden prominently, he was likely to make full use of his good draw (2.15). What is more he was still well treated on the evidence of his run at Lingfield on 6 June when he clocked a Topspeed rating of 100 (10lbs higher than his official rating of 90). This horse had all the key ingredients of a good bet. He was in form, he was one of the 'class' horses in the race, he was well handicapped, well drawn, had his ideal conditions of York, good ground and his trainer was in form. Incredibly he was on offer at 16-1 in the morning which was outstanding value. Fortunately there was a happy ending because Ice held on well to win by a length.

SIR JACK

20-1   19 June 2000, Windsor, 6F

The high numbers have the advantage at Windsor when the ground is riding fast so I began by eliminating stalls 1-10. Of the others, one was a three-year-old, one was blinkered for the first time, one had not won a handicap in 25 starts, one had not won a handicap in 45 starts, Ivory Dawn needed a downhill track and Slumbering needed further, so they were all eliminated. Of the four contenders, Sir Jack stood out. He was owned by the Lucayan Stud, who don't have many bad horses, and he had joined David Nicholls during the winter following a gelding operation. The horse looked very well handicapped to me. He had been dropped to the lowly rating of 56 following two fair runs in sellers on soft ground but had started 2000 on a mark of 80.

Last time out he had come a good fourth of 19 over seven furlongs at Redcar having had 'every chance' one furlong out despite an awful draw. He had been dropped 9lbs by the Handicapper following that solid performance which seemed very generous. David Nicholls had an excellent 33% strike rate at Windsor and the only horse he had sent down to the track was Sir Jack. Franny Norton had also been booked for the ride. A check of the entries for the race showed that Nicholls had entered three horses for the race but had chosen to rely on Sir Jack to do the business. He was well drawn in stall 17 (1.9) and appeared to have everything in his favour. I felt sure that he was about to take advantage of some very lenient handicapping and the 20-1 on offer in the morning was generous.

I backed him each way and fortunately he managed to sneak into fourth place having had no luck in running. The *Racing Post* reported that: 'The unlucky horse in the race was Sir Jack who travelled well against the stands rail but was denied a run until inside the final furlong.' The winner Nineacres went into my notebook as one to keep an eye on after managing to win from stall 3.

TUSSLE

20-1   *23 June 2000, Ascot, 6F, 'Wokingham Handicap'*

When analysing the major handicaps such as the Wokingham it is crucial to concentrate on the horses that have proven they can handle a large field of runners and that are guaranteed to stay the trip. These handicaps are invariably run at a furious pace from start to finish and they provide a searching test of a horse's stamina. I will only back a horse in this type of race if it has won over a longer trip in the past or has run well in a similar race. I tend to avoid fillies unless they have proven that they can handle the hurly-burly of a 30-runner 'cavalry charge'.

Normally the high numbers have the edge in the Wokingham and the results from the meeting earlier in the week suggested that the middle to high numbers would hold sway. I therefore eliminated stalls 1-12 and included among those axed was the forecast favourite Pepperdine. I also eliminated all the runners that were set to carry over nine stones, as weight usually has a significant effect in 30-runner handicaps of this class. Of the others, one needed softer ground, one was a three-year-old, one was blinkered for the first time, one was too old, one was having its first run of the season and two were best over five furlongs, so they were also eliminated. Of the remaining four Tussle stood out.

He looked well drawn in stall 17 and crucially he was definitely well enough handicapped to win such a competitive race. He was on a 7lbs lower handicap mark than when he finished an excellent fifth in the race the previous year, beaten just over two lengths despite having been drawn on the 'wrong' side of the track. He had some good form over seven, while he had proven that he had the necessary stamina and that he could also handle a big field of runners. Furthermore, in the *Racing Post* on 2 May, his trainer Michael Bell had said the following about his charge: 'His season is being geared around the Wokingham. We fancied him strongly last year when he won the race on the far side ... he hasn't been over-raced and looks to have progressed well. All roads lead to Ascot.'

This positive message provided me with an excellent pointer as I was able to totally disregard the horse's dismal showing on his only run of the season so far at Haydock when he had finished 17th of 19. *Raceform* reported that he had been 'backward' that day which was further evidence, if you needed it, that the horse was being aimed at the race today. Richard Quinn was a positive booking for the stable and I felt very confident that Tussle would run a big race. I backed the horse each way at 20-1 (to finish in the first five places) and he ran well to finish second, beaten by Harmonic Way who surprisingly managed to overcome the burden of 9-6 to supplement his win in the previous year's Stewards' Cup. The result once again confirmed the need for proven big-race form and stamina.

ACE OF PARKES

14-1   *28 June 2000, Chester, 5F*

It is crucial to be drawn low at Chester and any horse drawn higher than six faces a tough task. I therefore began by eliminating stalls 7-16. Of the remaining six I also eliminated the inexperienced three-year-old Look Here Now, who was dropping back in distance and was likely to find things happening too quickly in this competitive race. Of the others, I opted for Ace of Parkes who looked potentially well handicapped. He had been a useful two-year-old, winning three races, two by wide margins when making all, and he had twice been successful at the track. He had started his three-year-old campaign on a mark of 104 but, as so often happens with precocious two-year-olds, he failed to reproduce his juvenile form and by the beginning of 2000 he had been dropped to 85. It is not uncommon for a horse of this type to return to form at four, having matured physically, and this is what I anticipated.

Ace of Parkes had run well on his seasonal reappearance over course and distance, finishing fifth of 12 after starting slowly and meeting trouble in running, but admittedly disappointed somewhat next time with no obvious excuse. The result of that poor run was a lowering of his official rating by a further 2lbs and I felt that now, having had two runs to reach full fitness, he would be able to take advantage of some lenient handicapping. It is a big advantage to race prominently at Chester and I felt that he was likely to try to make all from his number 2 stall. I also liked the fact that the horse had an excellent wins to runs record of 20% and that his trainer Alan Berry was in good form. Ace of Parkes was on offer at 14-1 and in this 16-runner race I felt sure that he would make the first four so I backed him with confidence each way. Unfortunately, despite taking a keen hold the horse was not allowed to lead as I had anticipated and he finished a disappointing sixth. The winner was the top weight Damalis who broke well to lead from her number 3 stall and remained prominent throughout, surprising me in the process by reproducing her best form on the prevailing fast ground.

INDIAN SPARK

12-1   *15 July 2000, Chester, 5F, Listed*

I very rarely get involved in this type of race but when I saw that Indian Spark was running and that he had the plum draw of stall one I felt that I had found a good bet. On the face of it he had a stiff-looking task at the weights as he was officially rated 12lbs inferior to the course specialist Tedburrow and 9lbs below Proud Native. Furthermore, he had been running in handicaps earlier in the season and had started the campaign on the lowly mark of 76. He was now on a mark of 103 following some good runs in handicaps, but the bare evidence suggested that he was unlikely to be Listed class. After all, he had been well beaten when stepping up into a Listed race at Newcastle last time and had finished four lengths behind Tedburrow on the same weight terms. However, there were good reasons to believe that he was up to the task. Firstly, although the press did not seem to be aware of it, I knew that the horse had been gelded during the winter and that the operation had brought about considerable improvement. Secondly, I remembered that jockey Tony Culhane had expressed the opinion that Indian Spark had 'felt Group class' after the horse had won a competitive handicap by three lengths at York on 16 June and, if he was right, then the horse was up to Listed standard.

I am normally cautious about accepting what connections say about a horse at face value, but I had little doubt here, because Indian Spark had twice clocked Topspeed ratings of 113 which suggested that he was better than his mark of 103. Furthermore, Indian Spark's run behind Tedburrow last time was easily excused as he was not well drawn and did not appreciate the firm ground. Now that he had a better draw than Tedburrow (stall 5) and had his ideal soft ground I was confident that he would be able to turn the tables on the favourite. As an added bonus Indian Spark's trainer had an excellent 40% strike rate at the course and he clearly did not make the journey down from Scotland lightly. The 12-1 on offer early represented outstanding value but given the poor place odds on offer in this type of race I backed the horse to win only. He won nicely at 5-1 having apparently been heavily supported in the Scottish offices during the day.

NINEACRES

20-1   *15 July 2000, York, 6F*

Low to middle numbers had dominated the sprints here for some time so I began by eliminating stalls 13-23 and this dispensed with the favourite Friar Tuck. I also quickly eliminated the second favourite Downland who to my mind was clearly not a sprinter. I was able to eliminate a further eight of the well-drawn runners, which left only three contenders. Of these Nineacres just had to be backed at 20-1!

Despite being a nine-year-old he had been a revelation during the season, winning five races and improving from his previous highest winning turf mark of 42 to a current rating of 70. It is very unusual for a horse of his age to improve and I take my hat off to his excellent, but underrated, trainer Milton Bradley. I had made a note to follow Nineacres after he managed to win a handicap from a poor draw at Windsor earlier in the season. When I saw that he had clocked a Topspeed figure of 83 that day I knew that he was still well handicapped and that he was likely to win more races. He was well suited by the conditions and his trainer was in good form. When you find an in-form, improving, well-handicapped horse that is also advantageously drawn, available at odds of 20-1 you simply have to back it. I backed him each way and was rewarded after he came third, beaten by a neck having lost the lead near the finish.

PURE COINCIDENCE & MISS FIT
20-1 / 25-1   *16 July 2000, Haydock, 5F*

The middle to low numbers had held the advantage on Haydock's sprint course for some time so I began by eliminating stalls 11-19. Of the others, four were outclassed, Trinity had breathing problems and had never won a handicap and Bedevilled needed a stiffer track. Of the remaining four, both Miss Fit and Pure Coincidence had to be backed at what looked over-generous prices. Miss Fit was potentially 'thrown in' on her best form of last season being 16lbs below her highest winning mark. She had shown bits and pieces of form during the season but had not really fired. However, she usually does not come to hand until July and after her last run *Raceform* described her as having 'looked well' for the first time this season. On that occasion at Haydock she had run well for five of the race's six furlongs, despite being poorly drawn, which suggested that she was returning to form. She was well drawn today after being dropped a further 6lbs in the ratings and was returning to her ideal trip of five furlongs. The 25-1 on offer seemed far too big and I backed her each way.

Pure Coincidence also seemed well handicapped being 4lbs below his highest winning mark from 1999, and he had dropped 8lbs since the start of the season. He also looked to be coming to hand having 'looked well' when badly drawn last time out at Chester. He was now taking a big drop in class into a 0-80 handicap from a 0-95 handicap, his trainer was in good form and the horse looked poised to take advantage of some lenient handicapping from his good draw. Again 20-1 looked generous so I backed him each way as well. Although it is arguably not sensible to have four bets in one race, I felt confident that both of them would get placed. In the event Pure Coincidence was beaten one length into third having led until near the finish, but Miss Fit just missed out in fifth place. I won on the race, but not as much as I had anticipated!

EL GRAN PAPA
10-1   *29 July 2000, Ascot, 7F*

The winners of the three races run over the straight course the day before were drawn 2, 3 and 1 so I felt confident that the low numbers would dominate, and I began by eliminating stalls 6-24. Of the remaining five runners, El Gran Papa appealed the most. He was a lightly-raced, improving three-year-old, who looked well handicapped on a mark of 96 on the evidence of his win in the Britannia Handicap two runs earlier when he had clocked a Topspeed rating of 105. He had also won two races over a mile and had demonstrated that he had the necessary stamina to win this big-field handicap run over a testing seven furlongs. His trainer John Gosden was also in excellent form and had won this race last season so I felt that a big run from the horse was likely.

Although he was set to carry only 7-10 (usually a negative factor) he was only a three- year-old, so after taking weight-for-age into account (7lbs allowance) and con- sidering that the horse was probably better than his bare rating, judging by his Topspeed figures, I felt that he was unlikely to be outclassed here. My belief in the horse's chance was strengthened, after the first race of the day run on the straight course was won by the horse in stall 3. I backed him to win at 10-1 which I thought was a value price given that there were only a handful of runners in with a realistic chance of winning. In the event he came a good second, beaten a neck by Tillerman who was drawn in stall 2, and the pair were clear of the other runners.

BON AMI & BLUE MOUNTAIN
50-1 / 8-1   *5 August 2000, Goodwood, Stewards' Cup*

Traditionally the high numbers have the advantage in this race and all the evidence from earlier in the week suggested that they would today, so I began by eliminating stalls 1-18. Of the others, one had recently burst blood vessels, one had not won since 1998, one was too old, one needed softer ground, Alegria was badly handicapped, Alastair Smellie was totally out of form and both Tayseer and Second Wind needed further than six furlongs on this sharp track. Of the remainder Bon Ami looked to have a leading chance and was clearly overpriced at 50-1 (to finish in the first five for each-way backers). He was well handicapped having been lowered 9lbs by the Handicapper since coming second by a short head in the Great St Wilfrid Handicap at Ripon in 1999 and now had a good 5lbs claimer riding. He had also come a good third in the Stewards' Cup trial race over course and distance earlier in the season therefore demonstrating a liking for big-field handicaps, and he had been placed both times he had run at Goodwood. Last time out he had finished 13th of 19 at Ascot but had a poor draw so the run could be ignored. Prior to that he had put in several good performances and from a good draw and with conditions to suit, I felt he was likely to run well here. I backed him each way.

Blue Mountain also seemed the ideal type for this race. He was very consistent with a strike rate of 25% and was open to further improvement. He had the necessary stamina as he had previously been campaigned over longer distances and he had done well since dropping back to six furlongs, winning both the handicaps he had competed in over the distance. He looked reasonably treated being only 4lbs higher than when he won the Stewards' Cup trial earlier in the season, despite having been hampered at the start, and he had conditions in his favour today. From his good draw I felt that he just about represented value at 8-1 and I backed him to win. In the event he ran dismally, never getting into the race, but Bon Ami ran a blinder to finish second, looking all over the winner until Richard Hughes on Tayseer came fast and late to deny him, demonstrating once again what a test of stamina these big handicaps are. I felt pretty sick, particularly as Hughes had similarly denied me victory in the Wokingham at Ascot. Still, the place element of the bet paid 11 and a half to one and I suppose I got a decent enough return!

STRONG PRESENCE
9-1   *28 August 2000, Ripon, 8F*

I think that this was one of the best bets I placed during the season. I had winners at much bigger prices but this one gave me a lot of satisfaction because it was mainly down to intuition and reading between the lines. It is always hard to assess a horse that is having its first run in a handicap, particularly when it has had only two or three racecourse appearances. The Handicapper has very little evidence to draw on when allocating these horses a rating and it is not surprising that many turn out to be either very well, or poorly handicapped. I emphasise 'turn out' because it is usually only after a horse has run in a handicap or two that this becomes apparent. When I was analysing this race I became convinced that Strong Presence had been underrated by the Handicapper and that he was 'thrown in' on this his handicap debut.

Strong Presence was a three-year-old colt who had only run three times, his form figures reading 5-12. He was now having his first run in a handicap. Postmark of the *Racing Post* considered that he was the second worst handicapped horse in the race and rated him 10lbs inferior to the four joint top-rated. However, there were numerous clues that indicated that the horse was in fact well handicapped. The horse was owned and trained by Tom Tate who is normally associated with National Hunt horses and it was therefore interesting that his owner/trainer had decided to run him on the Flat. The horse had only run once as a two-year-old, making his debut in November in a competitive Class D Maiden at Doncaster. Significantly, particularly given that he was trainer-owned, he was backed from 40-1 into 16-1, and he went some way towards justifying that support by finishing a good fifth of 20 runners, beating the sixth horse by five lengths. He did not run again until he competed in a four-runner Class D Newmarket Maiden on 21 July and he was once again well backed from 7-1 into 4-1, but this time he justified the support, winning by a head. He led early in the race before being headed one furlong out, but rallied gamely to lead again near the finish and demonstrated in the process that a longer trip would probably prove ideal. *Raceform* noted that Strong Presence 'had done well' physically over the winter. In other words he had developed into a strong-looking individual. Although that race appeared to have been fairly uncompetitive, having been contested by only four runners, closer inspection revealed that this had not been the case. The *Racing Post*'s 'Racecheck' feature showed that the other three horses had gone on to win one race and to be placed on three occasions. None had been unplaced and in fact it was the fourth-placed horse Whistler that went on to win a Class D Maiden at Salisbury from a poor draw.

Following his win Strong Presence was allocated an official rating of 80 and on his third run he competed in a six-furlong, Class D, 0-80 classified stakes for horses aged three and over at Ayr. Strong Presence did well to finish a close second to the improving and older Abbajabba, again 'keeping on' at the finish having not had much room in the final furlong, and finishing over four lengths in front of the fourth horse.

His trainer had now decided to enter the horse in a handicap for the first time and, significantly, to also step him up in trip from six to eight furlongs. Not only had all three of his runs suggested that he would be suited by further than six furlongs but his breeding also indicated that he would be well served by a mile. The *Racing Post's* form guide for the horse showed that the offspring of his sire Anshan had a median winning distance of 8.1F, so sprinting was unlikely to be his forte. I felt sure that he would improve for the step up in distance. I also noted that Terry Lucas was again riding the horse having partnered it every other time it had run. What made this interesting was that Lucas rides for Mick Easterby who had two runners in the race, including the eventual 9-2 favourite Pension Fund. Although I was only guessing, I felt it likely that, knowing Strong Presence's potential, Lucas had sought permission from his boss to ride the horse instead of one of the stable's runners. As an added bonus the horse had a good draw in stall 9 of 12, given that he was likely to race prominently. I backed the horse to win at 9-1 and he won comfortably despite pulling very hard early on in the race, which showed how well handicapped he was.

LADY BOXER

33-1 *16 September 2000, Ayr, 6F*

On the evidence of the earlier races at the meeting the middle of the course was probably favoured but I felt that any advantage would be slight. I decided to concentrate on those drawn middle to high. With the ground riding 'soft with heavy patches' and with a fast pace guaranteed in this 29-runner race, I knew that the key to success would be proven stamina. I decided therefore that I would concentrate on those horses that had previously won over at least seven furlongs. By combining this rule with the elimination of the horses drawn 1-10, I narrowed the field down to just five contenders.

Of those five Lady Boxer stood out at the available odds of 33-1. She had won two races out of four on soft ground and crucially she had won over an extended seven furlongs at Chester two runs earlier in a much higher-class race, confirming that she had the necessary stamina. She had also clocked a Topspeed rating of 79 on that occasion which suggested that she was well enough handicapped on a current official rating of 74. The clincher for me was that she had finished fourth in the race last year as a three-year-old, despite having been badly drawn, and had proven that although she was a filly she could cope with a huge field of runners. I became convinced that she would run a big race and that 33-1 represented outstanding value. I backed her each way and she landed the spoils, staying on strongly in the final furlong to lead in the last strides when others were tiring badly.

TOMMY SMITH

20-1 *25 August 2001, Beverley, 5F*

Only the highest five stalls have positive draw figures in these sprints so I began by eliminating all the runners drawn six or more away from the inside rail. This season the draw seemed to be having even more influence than usual with 50% of the 18 races to date having been won by horses housed in one of the highest three stalls and I felt pretty confident that one of them would be successful today.

Of the remaining five contenders the first to go was American Cousin who was invariably held up for a late run in his races. As a result he was sure to surrender the advantage of his plum draw in stall 20 to the prominent horses and hold up types have a desperate record in 5F races at Beverley **(0.3).** Ravishing was usually held up as well and she was also a filly – a negative factor in August. Furthermore, last time out she ran over course and distance but failed to win from stall 19 of 20 so I could see no reason why she would win from stall 15 today, especially as she had been raised 3lbs in the ratings since. The 8-year-old Blessingindisguise was clearly on the downgrade, having dropped from an official rating of 100 to just 67 over the course of the previous two seasons. He had become too inconsistent to merit an interest at 6-1 here having won just once in 20 races during the last two years. I also eliminated Hilton Head who I felt would prefer softer ground and anyway fillies have a poor record in August. Diamond Geezer had to go also. He was definitely better off over six furlongs and he looked poorly handicapped now after having been raised 5lbs for coming second twice recently. He appeared vulnerable, given that his official rating was 8lbs above his last winning mark, especially as he was a 5-year-old and there was no obvious reason why he might improve.

This left Tommy Smith who was well drawn in stall 19. The key to this gelding appeared to be fast ground and he had won three races form 12 starts when conditions underfoot were in his favour. He had been in good form earlier in the season but then started slowly in three consecutive races and finished well beaten on each occasion. This prompted his trainer to reapply a visor at Redcar on 22 July. This was the second time the gelding had been equipped with the headgear. He had unsuccessfully worn a visor as a 2-year-old but an assessment of its effect on his performance that day was impossible because his chance had been ruined by prevailing soft ground. On this occasion it clearly had the desired effect and Tommy Smith broke smartly and made all to win convincingly, beating 21 other runners by a length.

Since then the gelding had raced twice more but on both occasion he finished last and it was these two dismal showings that had resulted in him being on offer at 20-1 today. However, both runs were excusable and should have been ignored. He had been drawn on the wrong side of the track at Nottingham and hated the soft ground there and next time at Pontefract his saddle slipped and he was virtually pulled up. He now had everything in his favour again for the first time since his Redcar victory. If he was able to take an early lead as expected from stall 19, he was sure to be hard to catch. Several good Topspeed figures suggested that he was well enough handicapped, particularly if the visor had brought about some improvement which seemed likely from the available evidence. In the event, the only real contender made most and kept on strongly from Ravishing to win at very rewarding odds.

ABBAJABA

20-1   *13 October 2001, York, 6F*

The middle to low draws are strongly favoured on the straight course at York and the advantage they enjoy is most pronounced when the ground is good to soft or softer. I had little doubt that the low numbers would dominate the race, particularly as the old speedster Lago Di Varano was sure to take the farside along at a good pace from his number eight draw. I therefore began by eliminating stalls 12 to 23. Of the others Juwwi and Seven No Trumps needed faster ground. Marweh had not reappeared until 4 August this season and had obviously had training problems in view of the fact that he had been wearing leg bandages in his three races since. Heathyard Blessing was another who had training problems as he had only run once last season and three times this year. He had also failed to take advantage of his plum stall 20 draw at Beverley last time out. Lago Di Varano is better over 5F when the ground is soft. Armanagac was also eliminated because he had run below form on his last two outings without apparent explanations and after 12 runs he seemed to have had enough for the season. Tom Tun was also given the chop because his record suggested that he was not quite up to winning a race of this class.

This left only four contenders. Of these Abbajaba made most appeal and just had to be backed at 20-1. During the previous season he had improved considerably and become very consistent, winning three of his eight starts and finishing unplaced on only one occasion. The key to him was soft ground and since the start of the 2000 season his record on ground good/soft or softer was 4, 2, 1, 1, 2, 2, 5. His obvious preference for soft ground had led his trainer to give him a mid-season break and the same tactic had been employed in 2001. Fairhurst's plan was to freshen the gelding up before having a tilt at the Ayr Gold Cup.

On his return from a 104-day break, Abbajaba demonstrated his well-being when coming an excellent third in the Great St Wilfrid handicap at Ripon despite being disadvantaged by a low draw. He then predictably finished unplaced on fast ground at Doncaster before heading to Ayr for his intended target. Unfortunately for connections, their careful plans were scuppered by the unseasonably firm ground at Ayr and Abbajaba was also handicapped by an unfavourable draw. He never got into the race. And so to the recovery mission! The ground had finally come right for the gelding and he had also landed the plum draw (**4.4**). He looked well enough handicapped, having previously recorded Topspeed figures of 92 and 93. With everything in his favour I felt confident that he would reproduce his best form. Following two excusable defeats since his eye-catching Ripon run, he was on offer at the very generous odds of 20-1 and looked outstanding value.

My one concern was that he was usually held up in his races. This is normally a bit of a disadvantage at York, but given that there were several front runners in the race and that the conditions were testing I felt sure that 20-1 more than compensated for the doubts I had on that score. In the event he won nicely. The first four home were drawn 6, 2, 1 and 8; the first and second came from off the pace to contest the lead inside the final furlong.

CONCLUSION

Having regularly written letters to *Raceform Update*'s Sports Forum over the last few years, I have learned that many punters take some persuading that backing horses at long odds is a viable strategy. I have come in for my fair share of criticism for daring to suggest that it can be viable! Contributing to Sports Forum has been a bit frustrating at times. Space constraints mean that letters have to be kept short and it is a challenge to get your point across comprehensively when trying to keep a letter as brief as possible. It was this sense of frustration that led me to write this book and I trust that I have been able to produce a fuller and therefore a more understandable explanation of my beliefs and the reasoning behind them. If I have managed to persuade some of you to drop your systematic methods, or if I have challenged your belief that picking as many winners as possible is the sole route to success, then the book will have been worthwhile. I hope that you feel inspired to put some, if not all, of the ideas to the test. If you do, remember, the harder you work at this game the luckier you become!

APPENDIX A

PACE FIGURES

The pace figures contained in the following charts have been calculated using data from handicap races run on turf during the last five seasons.

The MID-DIVISION AND BEHIND group makes up 50% of the runners in a race on average. Therefore, when this group boasts a win ratio of more than 1.0 it is the dominant group and the majority of winners are held up for a late challenge. The LED AND PROMINENT group and the CHASED LEADERS group account for 26% and 24% of the runners respectively and it is not until they have pace figures of approximately 2.0 or more that they account for the majority of winners.

ASCOT

DISTANCES	MID-DIVISION AND BEHIND	CHASED LEADERS	LED PROMINENT
5F & 6F	0.7	0.7	2.0
7F & 8F	1.0	0.5	1.4
10F & 12F	1.1	0.7	1.2
16F+	1.4	0.5	0.7

AYR

DISTANCES	MID-DIVISION AND BEHIND	CHASED LEADERS	LED PROMINENT
5F & 6F	0.8	1.1	1.4
7F & 8F	0.7	1.2	1.4
9F+	1.0	1.2	0.9

BATH

DISTANCES	MID-DIVISION AND BEHIND	CHASED LEADERS	LED PROMINENT
5F & 5F 161Y	1.3	0.6	0.8
8F, 10F, 11F	1.1	1.0	0.9
13F & 17F	1.1	0.9	0.9

BEVERLEY

DISTANCES	MID-DIVISION AND BEHIND	CHASED LEADERS	LED PROMINENT
5F	0.3	1.8	1.7
7F & 8F	0.6	1.7	1.1
10F+	0.9	1.3	1.0

BRIGHTON

DISTANCES	MID-DIVISION AND BEHIND	CHASED LEADERS	LED PROMINENT
5F & 6F	0.7	0.8	1.9
7F & 8F	0.8	1.0	1.4
10F+	0.9	0.9	1.3

CARLISLE

DISTANCES	MID-DIVISION AND BEHIND	CHASED LEADERS	LED PROMINENT
5F & 6F	0.9	0.9	1.2
7F & 8F	0.8	1.2	1.2
9F+	0.6	1.0	1.7

CATTERICK

DISTANCES	MID-DIVISION AND BEHIND	CHASED LEADERS	LED PROMINENT
5F & 6F	0.3	1.5	1.8
7F	0.8	1.2	1.1
12F+	1.0	1.3	0.8

CHEPSTOW

DISTANCES	MID-DIVISION AND BEHIND	CHASED LEADERS	LED PROMINENT
5F & 6F	0.7	0.5	2.1
7F & 8F	0.7	0.4	2.2
10F+	1.0	0.7	1.3

CHESTER

DISTANCES	MID-DIVISION AND BEHIND	CHASED LEADERS	LED PROMINENT
5F & 6F	0.4	0.5	2.6
7F, 7F 122Y	0.5	1.4	1.6
9F+	0.8	1.4	1.1

DONCASTER

DISTANCES	MID-DIVISION AND BEHIND	CHASED LEADERS	LED PROMINENT
5F, 6F, 7F, 8F	0.7	1.6	1.0
8F (ROUND)	1.3	1.0	0.3
10F, 11F, 12F	0.9	1.4	0.7
14F+	1.5	0.4	0.6

Doncaster 8F (Round) data based on limited evidence.

EPSOM

DISTANCES	MID-DIVISION AND BEHIND	CHASED LEADERS	LED PROMINENT
5F & 6F	0.7	0.5	1.9
7F & 8F 114Y	0.9	0.9	1.4
10F+	1.1	0.3	1.5

FOLKESTONE

DISTANCES	MID-DIVISION AND BEHIND	CHASED LEADERS	LED PROMINENT
5F, 6F, 7F	0.6	0.6	2.1
6F 110Y & 9F	0.6	0.7	1.9
12F+	1.0	0.5	1.4

GOODWOOD

DISTANCES	MID-DIVISION AND BEHIND	CHASED LEADERS	LED PROMINENT
5F & 6F	0.9	0.7	1.4
7F & 8F	0.8	1.0	1.4
9F & 10F	1.0	0.6	1.3
12F+	1.3	0.8	0.7

HAMILTON

DISTANCES	MID-DIVISION AND BEHIND	CHASED LEADERS	LED PROMINENT
5F & 6F	0.3	1.6	1.7
8F & 9F	0.8	0.9	1.5
11F+	1.0	0.9	1.1

HAYDOCK

DISTANCES	MID-DIVISION AND BEHIND	CHASED LEADERS	LED PROMINENT
5F & 6F	0.9	0.9	1.3
7F & 8F	0.9	1.3	1.0
10F+	1.0	1.1	0.8

KEMPTON

DISTANCES	MID-DIVISION AND BEHIND	CHASED LEADERS	LED PROMINENT
5F & 6F	0.8	0.9	1.6
7F, 8F & 10F (JUB)	0.8	1.3	1.1
7F, 8F & 9F (ROUND)	0.9	0.9	1.4
12F+	1.2	0.5	1.0

LEICESTER

DISTANCES	MID-DIVISION AND BEHIND	CHASED LEADERS	LED PROMINENT
5F & 6F	0.8	1.0	1.4
7F & 8F	0.8	0.8	1.6
10F+	0.9	0.8	1.4

LINGFIELD (TURF)

DISTANCES	MID-DIVISION AND BEHIND	CHASED LEADERS	LED PROMINENT
5F & 6F	0.6	1.1	1.7
7F & 7F 140Y	0.8	0.9	1.5
9F+	0.8	0.8	1.7

MUSSELBURGH

DISTANCES	MID-DIVISION AND BEHIND	CHASED LEADERS	LED PROMINENT
5F	0.4	1.0	2.2
7F & 8F	0.7	1.1	1.5
9F+	0.5	1.3	1.7

NEWBURY

DISTANCES	MID-DIVISION AND BEHIND	CHASED LEADERS	LED PROMINENT
5F & 6F	1.1	0.7	0.9
7F & 8F (STRAIGHT)	1.2	0.7	0.9
7F & 8F (ROUND)	0.9	0.9	1.3
9F & 10F	1.1	0.8	1.0
12F	1.3	0.6	0.8

When the ground is heavy prominent horses usually do best at Newbury.

NEWCASTLE

DISTANCES	MID-DIVISION AND BEHIND	CHASED LEADERS	LED PROMINENT
5F & 6F	0.4	1.7	1.4
7F & 8F (STRAIGHT)	0.7	1.4	1.3
8F & 9F (ROUND)	0.8	2.1	0.5
10F+	0.7	1.7	1.0

NEWMARKET (ROWLEY)

DISTANCES	MID-DIVISION AND BEHIND	CHASED LEADERS	LED PROMINENT
5F & 6F	0.5	1.1	1.7
7F, 8F & 9F	0.7	1.3	1.3
10F+	1.2	0.8	0.8

NEWMARKET (JULY)

DISTANCES	MID-DIVISION AND BEHIND	CHASED LEADERS	LED PROMINENT
5F & 6F	0.7	1.3	1.3
7F & 8F	1.1	0.9	1.0
10F+	0.9	1.0	1.2

NOTTINGHAM

DISTANCES	MID-DIVISION AND BEHIND	CHASED LEADERS	LED PROMINENT
5F & 6F	0.8	1.4	1.0
8F & 10F	0.9	0.9	1.2
12F+	1.1	1.0	0.8

Nottingham 5F & 6F data based on limited evidence.

PONTEFRACT

DISTANCES	MID-DIVISION AND BEHIND	CHASED LEADERS	LED PROMINENT
5F & 6F	0.7	1.0	1.4
8F & 10F	1.1	0.9	0.8
12F+	1.3	0.9	0.6

REDCAR

DISTANCES	MID-DIVISION AND BEHIND	CHASED LEADERS	LED PROMINENT
5F & 6F	0.4	1.4	1.8
7F & 8F	0.8	1.2	1.2
9F+	1.0	1.3	0.7

RIPON

DISTANCES	MID-DIVISION AND BEHIND	CHASED LEADERS	LED PROMINENT
5F & 6F	0.4	1.6	1.7
8F, 9F & 10F	0.7	1.1	1.5
12F+	0.8	1.5	1.0

SALISBURY

DISTANCES	MID-DIVISION AND BEHIND	CHASED LEADERS	LED PROMINENT
5F & 6F	0.7	1.1	1.4
7F & 8F	0.9	1.0	1.1
9F 198Y+	1.0	0.6	1.4

SANDOWN

DISTANCES	MID-DIVISION AND BEHIND	CHASED LEADERS	LED PROMINENT
5F	0.8	0.5	1.9
7F & 8F	1.1	0.7	1.1
9F & 10F	1.0	1.0	1.0
11F+	1.0	0.9	1.1

THIRSK

DISTANCES	MID-DIVISION AND BEHIND	CHASED LEADERS	LED PROMINENT
5F & 6F	0.5	1.3	1.7
7F & 8F	0.7	1.7	1.0
12F+	0.9	1.2	1.0

WARWICK

DISTANCES	MID-DIVISION AND BEHIND	CHASED LEADERS	LED PROMINENT
5F & 6F	0.5	0.8	2.1
6F 168Y & 8F	0.9	0.6	1.4
10F+	0.9	0.8	1.4

WINDSOR

DISTANCES	MID-DIVISION AND BEHIND	CHASED LEADERS	LED PROMINENT
5F & 6F	0.6	0.8	1.9
8F	0.8	1.1	1.4
10F+	0.9	0.8	1.3

YARMOUTH

DISTANCES	MID-DIVISION AND BEHIND	CHASED LEADERS	LED PROMINENT
5F & 6F	0.9	0.8	1.4
7F & 8F	0.7	0.7	1.8
10F+	1.0	0.7	1.3

YORK

DISTANCES	MID-DIVISION AND BEHIND	CHASED LEADERS	LED PROMINENT
5F & 6F	0.5	1.6	1.3
7F, 8F & 9F	0.8	1.5	0.8
10F+	1.0	1.0	1.0

APPENDIX B

DRAW FIGURES

When referring to the draw charts remember that where the stalls position is shown as LOW, stall one in the chart refers to stall number one in the race, but where the stalls position is described as HIGH, stall one refers to the highest numbered stall in the race and stall two refers to the second highest stall and so on.

The draw figures are calculated using data from the last five seasons. Of course the bias at a track can change from one season to another and the charts therefore include information designed to highlight those changes that became apparent during 2001. Firstly, the stalls that performed best during 2001 have been shaded grey and where the shaded stalls are grouped fairly close together their position shows where the bias lay. Beneath the average figures that appear in bold the previous average figures are shown in brackets. The difference between the two figures can be used to measure the extent of any change in the bias that occurred last season. If you wish, you can obtain approximate average figures for the 2001 season by calculating the difference between the new average figures in bold and the old average figures in brackets and multiplying by five.

Although the figures incorporate the results from the last five seasons there are nevertheless some that are based on limited evidence. Certain tracks stage less racing than others and their long-distance handicaps in particular tend to be few and far between. There is little point producing draw figures for each stall in these circumstances because they are unlikely to be reliable. Therefore, where the figures are based on limited evidence I have produced the 'average figures' only. I have not produced any figures at all for some distances at certain courses either because there was simply too little data to use or because the distance was two miles or more and there was no identifiable bias.

On some round courses such as Doncaster and Newbury the horses drawn wide in big fields usually do best when the going is soft or heavy. The ground near the inside running rail tends to become badly cut up and those racing wide on the better ground have the advantage. Of course the ground only becomes cut up near the inside rail after it has been raced on and in the early stages of a season the advantage held by the wide draws may not become apparent until after the first one or two meetings.

ASCOT

DISTANCES 5F, 6F, 7F, 8F (STRAIGHT COURSE)			DISTANCES 10F, 12F			DISTANCES 16F, 20F		
STALLS	LOW		STALLS	HIGH		STALLS	HIGH	
1	1.3		1	0.3		1	1.6	
2	1.5		2	0.8		2	3.0	
3	1.9		3	0.9	**0.7**	3	1.6	**1.7**
4	0.3	**1.1**	4	0.6	(0.76)	4	0.8	(1.82)
5	1.4	(1.13)	5	0.9		5	1.3	
6	0.9		6	1.7		6	0	
7	1.0		7	1.1		7	0.5	
8	0.4		8	0.7	**0.9**	8	0	**0.6**
9	0.7		9	0.5	(0.94)	9	0.8	(0.61)
10	1.2		10	1.0		10	1.6	
11	1.0		11	1.3		11	1.0	
12	0.4	**0.8**	12	4.9		12	3.1	
13	1.0	(0.81)	13	1.3	**2.2**	13	0	**1.1**
14	0.8		14	1.8	(1.94)	14	1.0	(0.61)
15	1.5		15	1.1		15	1.9	
16	0.5		16	3.3		16	0	
17	1.1		17	0		17	0	
18	0		18	0	**1.1**	18	0	
19	2.0		19	0	(1.06)	19	0	
20	0.8	**0.9**	20	0		20	0	
21	0.8	(1.01)				21	0	
22	1.8					22	4	**0.4**
23	0					23	0	(0.56)
24	0					24	0	
25	0					25	0	
26	0					26	0	
27	0					27	0	
28	3.7	**1.4**				28	0	
29	1.2	(1.13)				29	0	
30	5							
31+	0							

ASCOT (STRAIGHT COURSE) – On soft or heavy ground the high numbers usually enjoy a big advantage.

AYR

DISTANCES 5F, 6F			DISTANCE 7F			DISTANCES 8F, 9F 20y			DISTANCES 10F, 10F 192y		
STALLS	HIGH		STALLS	LOW		STALLS	LOW		STALLS	LOW	
1	1.4		1	0.4		1	1.7		1	0.3	
2	1.2	**1.0**	2	0.8		2	1.4	**1.2**	2	0.9	**0.9**
3	1.1	(1.03)	3	0.8	**0.8**	3	1.8	(1.13)	3	0.6	(0.87)
4	0.7		4	1.2	(0.93)	4	0.5		4	1.4	
5	0.7		5	0.8		5	0.5		5	1.5	
6	1.0		6	0.7		6	1.3		6	2.4	
7	1.1	**0.9**	7	1.5		7	1.3	**0.8**	7	1.2	**1.0**
8	1.3	(1.02)	8	0.4		8	0.5	(1.08)	8	0.9	(1.03)
9	0.6		9	1.9	**1.4**	9	0.8		9	0	
10	0.6		10	2.5	(1.24)	10	0.6		10	0	
11	0.8		11	2.0		11	0.7		11	1.1	
12	0.9	**0.6**	12	0		12	0.6	**0.7**	12	0	**1.3**
13	0.3	(0.36)	13	1.0		13	1.6	(0.52)	13	1.61	(1.42)
14	0.4		14	1.7		14	0		14	3.1	
15	0.5		15	0	**0.8**	15	0		15	2.3	
16	0.8		16	0	(0.74)	16	0		16	0	
17	1.7	**1.8**	17	0		17	0	**0.5**	17	0	
18	2.2	(1.92)	18	4.0		18	2.2	(0.57)	18	0	**0**
19	2.3					19	0		19	0	(0)
20	1.8					20	0		20	0	
21	2.0										
22	2.2										
23	0										
24	0	**0.9**									
25	0	(0.9)									
26	1.3										
27	2.0										
28	0										
29	0										
30	0										

AYR 5F & 6F – During the Gold Cup meeting check the early results to determine which side of the course is favoured.

BATH

DISTANCES 5F 11y, 5F 161y			DISTANCES 7F, 8F 5y			DISTANCES 10F 46y, 11F 44y		
STALLS	LOW		STALLS	LOW		STALLS	HIGH	
1	0.5		1	0.7		1	0.8	
2	0.8		2	1.4		2	1.2	
3	1.1	**1.0**	3	1.2	**1.2**	3	0	**1.4**
4	0.8	(0.94)	4	1.6	(1.15)	4	2.4	(1.55)
5	1.4		5	1.2		5	1.2	
6	0.6		6	0.9		6	2.8	
7	0.8		7	1.2		7	0.8	
8	1.7	**1.0**	8	1.4		8	0	
9	1.2	(1.09)	9	0.5	**0.7**	9	0	**0.9**
10	0.8		10	0	(0.76)	10	2.3	(0.75)
11	1.1		11	0		11	1.5	
12	0.8		12	1.1		12	1.6	
13	0	**0.9**	13	0.7		13	0	
14	2.0	(0.77)	14	1.3		14	0	
15	0.7		15	1.0	**1.0**	15	0	**0**
16	1.3		16	0.6	(1.10)	16	0	(0)
17	1.5		17	1.2		17	0	
18	1.9	**1.5**	18	1.6		18	0	
19	1.9	(1.90)						
20	0							

BATH 5F 11y, 5F 161y – Low numbers do as well as the high numbers when the stalls are placed HIGH.

BEVERLEY

DISTANCE 5F			DISTANCES 7F 100y, 8F 100y			DISTANCE 9F 207y			DISTANCES 11F 216y, 16F 35y		
STALLS	HIGH		STALLS	HIGH		STALLS	HIGH		STALLS		HIGH
1	3.0		1	1.7		1	1.7		1	0.7	
2	1.9	**2.5**	2	1.5		2	1.2		2	0.3	
3	2.2	(2.38)	3	1.3	**1.4**	3	1.3	**1.2**	3	1.3	**1.0**
4	3.2		4	1.0	(1.45)	4	1.1	(1.28)	4	1.5	(0.84)
5	2.0		5	1.4		5	0.8		5	0.5	
6	0.5		6	1.4		6	1.4		6	1.8	
7	0.8	**0.3**	7	1.4		7	1.1		7	0.8	
8	0	(0.25)	8	0.7		8	0.5		8	1.0	
9	0		9	0.6	**0.7**	9	0.5	**0.8**	9	1.4	**1.0**
10	0.3		10	0.7	(0.73)	10	1.4	(0.8)	10	1.7	(1.15)
11	0		11	0		11	1.3		11	0	
12	0.6	**0.10**	12	0.8		12	0		12	0.7	
13	0	(0.16)	13	0.2		13	2.4		13	2.1	
14	0		14	0.8		14	0.4		14	0.8	
15	0		15	0.7	**0.4**	15	0.4	**0.8**	15	0.5	
16	2.0		16	0	(0.25)	16	0	(0.72)	16	0	**0.5**
17	0		17	0		17	0		17	0	(0.5)
18	0	**0.7**	18	0		18	0		18	0	
19	0	(0.83)				19	0.9		19	0	
20	0										

BEVERLEY 5F – When the ground is soft or heavy the horses drawn low in large fields can sometimes gain an advantage by racing against the stands rail, but this is not a hard and fast rule.

BRIGHTON

DISTANCES 5F 59y, 5F 213y			DISTANCE 6F 209y			DISTANCE 7F 214y			DISTANCES 9F 209y, 11F 196y		
STALLS	LOW		STALLS	LOW		STALLS	LOW		STALLS	LOW	
1	1.3		1	0.4		1	0		1	1.3	
2	1.3		2	1.1		2	0.6	**0.6**	2	1.2	
3	0.9	**1.2**	3	0.8	**0.9**	3	1.1	(0.59)	3	0.3	**1.0**
4	1.4	(1.24)	4	1.0	(0.86)	4	0.8		4	1.1	(0.94)
5	1.7		5	1.3		5	0.8	**0.8**	5	1.1	
6	0.8		6	0.6		6	1.1	(1.18)	6	1.8	
7	0.6		7	1.1		7	0.8		7	0.5	
8	0.6		8	1.4		8	0.5	**0.8**	8	1.1	**1.0**
9	1.0	**0.7**	9	1.1	**0.9**	9	1.1	(0.74)	9	1.0	(1.09)
10	0.3	(0.72)	10	1.6	(0.88)	10	0.6		10	0.6	
11	1.1		11	0.4		11	1.4	**0.8**	11	0.3	
12	0.7		12	0.5		12	0.5	(0.52)	12	1.6	
13	0		13	1.0		13	2.4		13	0.8	**0.9**
14	0.4		14	1.2		14	2.4	**2.9**	14	0.7	(0.92)
15	0	**0.6**	15	0.7	**0.9**	15	4	(3.15)	15	0.7	
16	1.7	(0.46)	16	1.6	(0.85)				16	0.9	
17	0.6		17	0					17	0	
18	4		18	0					18	2.2	**1.0**
									19	0	(0.91)
									20	2.7	

BRIGHTON 7F 214y – The advantage enjoyed by the highest few stalls is probably caused by the bend in the 'straight' between the 8F and the 6F poles.

CARLISLE

DISTANCES 5F, 5F 207y			DISTANCES 6F 206y, 7F 214y			DISTANCE 9F 61y		
STALLS	*HIGH*		*STALLS*	*HIGH*		*STALLS*	*HIGH*	
1	1.0		1	1.3		1		
2	1.4		2	1.3		2		
3	1.9	**1.3**	3	0.3	**0.9**	3	**1.6**	
4	1.4		4	0.7		4		
5	1.0		5	0.6		5		
6	1.4		6	1.0		6		
7	1.0		7	1.3		7		
8	1.9	**1.0**	8	1.3		8		
9	0.5		9	1.9	**1.2**	9	**1.1**	
10	0		10	0.8		10		
11	1.1		11	0.9		11		
12	1.2		12	1.0		12		
13	0	**0.7**	13	0		13		
14	0		14	0.8		14		
15	1.1		15	1.0	**0.8**	15	**0.5**	
16	1.3		16	3.1		16		
17	0		17	0				
18	0	**1.0**	18	0				
19	0							
20	5							

There were no races run at Carlisle during 2001 owing to foot and mouth.

CATTERICK

DISTANCE 5F			DISTANCES 5F 212y, 7F			DISTANCES 11F 214y, 13F 175y		
STALLS	LOW		STALLS	LOW		STALLS	LOW	
1	0.8		1	0.7		1	1.5	
2	0		2	1.8		2	0.6	
3	1.2	**1.0**	3	0.8	**1.2**	3	1.2	**1.3**
4	0.8	(1.07)	4	1.1	(0.86)	4	2.4	(1.33)
5	1.6		5	0.8		5	1.5	
6	1.6		6	0.7		6	0.9	
7	1.3		7	0.9		7	0.9	
8	1.2	**1.0**	8	1.3	**1.0**	8	0.3	
9	0	(1.14)	9	1.3	(1.16)	9	0	**0.3**
10	0.5		10	0.9		10	0	(0.29)
11	0		11	0.5		11	0	
12	0.4		12	1.1		12	1.2	
13	1.3	**0.6**	13	0.3	**0.9**	13	1.9	
14	0	(0.42)	14	1.1	(0.94)	14	2.3	
15	1.5		15	1.7		15	0	**1.6**
16	4.1		16	2.0		16	2.8	(1.51)
17	0	**3.1**	17	0	**1.2**	17	0	
18	0	(3.45)	18	1.9	(1.42)	18	0	
19	5		19-20	0				

CATTERICK 5F – The advantage enjoyed by the high numbers in big fields is particularly strong on soft or heavy ground.

CHEPSTOW

DISTANCES 5F 16y, 6F 16y			DISTANCE 10F 36y		DISTANCES 12F 23y, 16F, 18F	
STALLS	*HIGH*		*STALLS*	*LOW*	*STALLS*	*LOW*
1	1.9		1		1	
2	1.2		2	**0.3**	2	
3	1.6	**1.3**	3	(0.32)	3	**1.1**
4	0.7	(1.12)	4		4	(1.1)
5	1.1		5		5	
6	0.5		6	**1.0**	6	
7	1.3		7	(0.79)	7	
8	1.0	**0.9**	8		8	
9	0.5	(1.02)	9		9	**0.8**
10	0.9		10	**1.4**	10	(0.81)
11	0.7		11	(1.56)	11	
12	1.8		12		12	
13	0.6	**1.0**	13		13	
14	1.1	(1.07)	14	**1.7**	14	
15	0.5		15	(1.68)	15	**1.2**
16	0		16		16	(1.2)
17	0				17	
18	0.6	**0.4**			18	
19	0.5	(0.35)				
20	1.5					

CHESTER

DISTANCES 5F 16y, 6F 18y			DISTANCES 7F 2y, 7F 122y			DISTANCES 10F 75y, 12F 66y			DISTANCES 13F, 15F 196y		
STALLS	LOW		STALLS	LOW		STALLS	LOW		STALLS	LOW	
1	2.5		1	1.5		1	1.8		1		
2	1.6	1.9	2	1.7	1.6	2	2.6	1.5	2		1.4
3	1.6	(1.84)	3	1.5	(1.93)	3	0.9	(1.55)	3		(1.44)
4	1.1		4	1.7		4	0.9		4		
5	1.1	1.5	5	1.4		5	1.7		5		
6	2.2	(1.61)	6	0.3	0.9	6	0.3	0.8	6		0.9
7	0		7	0.7	(0.7)	7	0.6	(0.73)	7		(0.57)
8	0.5	0.3	8	1.0		8	0.3		8		
9	0.4	(0.25)	9	0.8		9	0		9		
10	0		10	0.9	0.6	10	0		10		0.3
11	0		11	0	(0.42)	11	0.5		11		(0.37)
12	0.5	0.1	12	0.5		12	1.2	0.5	12		
13	0	(0)	13	0.5		13	2.2	(0.51)	13		
14	0		14	0		14	0		14		0
15	0		15	0	0.5	15	0		15		(0)
16	0		16	1.2	(0.4)	16	4		16		
			17	1.6							
			18	0							

DONCASTER

DISTANCES 5F, 6F, 7F, 8F GOOD GROUND TO HARD GROUND			DISTANCES 5F, 6F, 7F, 8F GOOD/SOFT GROUND TO HEAVY			DISTANCE 8F ROUND COURSE			DISTANCES 10F 60y, 11F, 12F GOOD GROUND TO HARD GROUND			DISTANCES 10F 60y, 11F, 12F GOOD/SOFT GROUND TO HEAVY		
STALLS	HIGH		STALLS	HIGH		STALLS	LOW		STALLS	LOW		STALLS	LOW	
1	1.6		1	2.8		1	2.0		1	1.8		1		
2	1.4		2	1.9		2	1.4		2	1.4		2		
3	1.0	**1.0**	3	0.5	**1.6**	3	2.5	**1.6**	3	1.7	**1.2**	3	**0.8**	
4	1.1	(1.12)	4	0.9	(1.56)	4	0.7	(1.49)	4	1.0	(0.96)	4	(0.57)	
5	0.8		5	1.4		5	1.3		5	0.2		5		
6	0.6		6	0.9		6	0.7		6	0.8		6		
7	0.7		7	0.5		7	1.1		7	2.2		7		
8	1.8		8	1.0	**0.4**	8	1.1	**0.9**	8	0.8	**1.2**	8	**1.1**	
9	1.5	**1.0**	9	0	(0.39)	9	0.7	(0.97)	9	1.0	(1.36)	9	(1.21)	
10	0.9	(0.96)	10	0		10	0.9		10	1.1		10		
11	0.8		11	0		11	0.6		11	1.0		11		
12	0.5		12	0		12	0.7		12	0.4		12		
13	0.9		13	0	**0**	13	0	**0.5**	13	0.4	**0.4**	13	**1.4**	
14	1.6		14	0	(0)	14	1.0	(0.52)	14	0	(0.52)	14	(1.32)	
15	1.0	**0.9**	15	0		15	0		15	0		15		
16	0.8	(0.83)	16	1.7		16	1.1		16	0.6		16		
17	1.3		17	3.0		17	0		17	2.6		17		
18	0		18	1.0	**1.9**	18	0		18	0	**(0.9)**	18	**0.5**	
19	1.1		19	1.0	(2.13)	19	0		19	0	(0.82)	19	(0.64)	
20	0.6		20	2.7		20	0	**0.3**	20	1.5		20		
21	0	**0.5**	21	3.0		21	0	(0.32)	21	1.8		21		
22	0	(0.64)	22	2.8	**3.0**	22	0		22	0		22		
23	0		23	2.5	(2.73)	23	0		23	0	**0.6**	23	**1.7**	
24	0		24	5		24	0		24	0	(0.76)	24	(2.08)	
									25	0		25		

DONCASTER 5F TO 8F (GOOD/SOFT TO HEAVY) – Although the bias is strong it can be hard to predict because either the low numbers or the high numbers can be favoured. The middle draws are at a big disadvantage in large fields. The 'pace' on each side of the track may influence the outcome.

EPSOM

DISTANCE 5F		DISTANCE 6F		DISTANCE 7F			DISTANCES 8F 114y, 10F 18y			DISTANCE 12F 10y		
STALLS	HIGH	STALLS	LOW	STALLS	LOW		STALLS	LOW		STALLS	LOW	
1		1		1	2.0		1	1.0		1	0.9	
2		2		2	0.5		2	1.4		2	0.3	
3	**1.4**	3	**0.8**	3	0.9	**1.4**	3	1.1	**1.1**	3	1.6	**1.0**
4	(1.53)	4	(0.82)	4	1.3	(1.56)	4	1.3	(1.18)	4	0.9	(1.19)
5		5		5	2.5		5	1.0		5	1.3	
6		6		6	0.9		6	0.6		6	1.3	
7		7		7	0		7	1.4		7	0.7	
8	**1.0**	8	**1.3**	8	0		8	0.6	**1.0**	8	1.3	**1.0**
9	(0.66)	9	(1.23)	9	0.9	**0.7**	9	1.0	(0.84)	9	1.4	(0.97)
10		10		10	1.5	(0.56)	10	0.9		10	0	
11		11		11	0		11	1.1		11	0.6	
12		12		12	2.4		12	0.5		12	2.5	
13	**0.3**	13		13	0		13	1.4	**1.1**	13	0	**1.1**
14	(0.36)	14	**1.2**	14	1.2		14	2.9	(1.33)	14	0	(0.82)
15		15	(0.89)	15	1.4	**0.8**	15	0		15	0	
16		16		16	0	(0.34)	16	0		16	4	
17	**0**	17		17	0		17	0		17	0	
18	(0)						18	0	**0**	18	0	
19							19	0	(0)	19	5	
							20	0		20	0	**0.9**
										21	0	(0.59)
										22	0	
										23	0	
										24	0	

FOLKESTONE

DISTANCE 5F, 6F, 7F (STRAIGHT COURSE) GOOD GROUND TO HARD GROUND		DISTANCES 5F, 6F, 7F (STRAIGHT COURSE) GOOD TO SOFT TO HEAVY GROUND		DISTANCE 6F 189y (ROUND COURSE)		DISTANCES 9F 149y, 12F, 15F 92y		
STALLS	LOW	STALLS	LOW	STALLS	HIGH	STALLS	HIGH	
1		1		1		1	1.2	
2	**1.0**	2	**0.4**	2	**1.4**	2	1.8	
3	(1.07)	3	(0.38)	3	(1.52)	3	1.2	**1.2**
4		4		4		4	1.1	(1.2)
5		5		5		5	1.1	
6		6	**0.4**	6		6	0.7	
7		7	(0.38)	7	**1.0**	7	1.0	
8		8		8	(0.95)	8	0.5	
9	**0.9**	9		9		9	0.9	**0.9**
10	(0.79)	10	**1.0**	10		10	0.9	(0.94)
11		11	(0.97)	11		11	1.5	
12		12		12		12	0.9	
13		13		13	**0.3**	13	0.3	
14		14	**3.0**	14		14	0.5	
15	**1.0**	15	(2.63)	15		15	0	**0.4**
16	(0.93)	16		16		16	0	(0.25)
17				17		17	2.4	
18						18	0	
19								

GOODWOOD

DISTANCES 5F, 6F		DISTANCES 7F, 8F		DISTANCES 9F, 9F 192y		DISTANCES 10F, 11F		DISTANCES 12F, 14F, 16F	
STALLS	LOW	STALLS	HIGH	STALLS	HIGH	STALLS	HIGH	STALLS	HIGH
1	1.3	1	2.4	1	1.7	1		1	2.3
2	1.2	2	2.0	2	1.5	2		2	2.3 **1.5**
3	0.5 **0.7**	3	1.5 **1.7**	3	0.9 *1.0*	3	**1.1**	3	0.8 (1.58)
4	0 (0.72)	4	1.4 (1.72)	4	0.9 (0.99)	4	(1.49)	4	1.7
5	0.6	5	1.2	5	0.3	5		5	0.3
6	1.0	6	0.9	6	0.6	6		6	1.4
7	0.6	7	0.7	7	0.9	7	**0.8**	7	0.3 **0.6**
8	1.8 **0.9**	8	1.0 **0.6**	8	0.3 **0.9**	8	(0.74)	8	0.4 (0.44)
9	0.7 (0.93)	9	0.4 (0.63)	9	1.2 (1.03)	9		9	0.2
10	0.4	10	0.2	10	1.7	10		10	0.2
11	0.6	11	0	11	1.2	11		11	0
12	0.8	12	1.1	12	1.6	12		12	3.4
13	1.4 **1.1**	13	0.4 **0.4**	13	2.4 **1.3**	13	**1.3**	13	0.3 **1.1**
14	1.4 (1.01)	14	0 (0.38)	14	0.7 (1.05)	14	(0.56)	14	0 (1.16)
15	1.3	15	0.6	15	0	15		15	0
16	1.3	16	1.2	16	0	16		16	4
17	3.2	17	0	17	0			17	0
18	2.2 **1.9**	18	1.0 **0.7**	18	2.0 **0.6**				
19	4.7 (1.83)	19	0 (0.91)	19	0 (0.8)				
20	0	20	0	20	2.7				
21	1.9	21	3.3						
22	0	22	0						
23	0								
24	0 **1.5**								
25	0 (1.76)								
26	0								
27	0								
28	4								
29	0								

GOODWOOD 5F & 6F The advantage held by the middle to high numbers is greatest when the ground is soft or heavy.

HAMILTON

STALLS	DISTANCES 5F, 6F HIGH		STALLS	DISTANCES 5F, 6F LOW		STALLS	DISTANCES 8F 65y, 9F 36y HIGH		STALLS	DISTANCES 11F 16y, 13F 9y, 12F 17y LOW	
1	2.5		1	0.2		1	1.4		1	0.4	
2	1.5		2	0.8		2	1.9		2	1.2	
3	2.0	**1.6**	3	0.6	**0.6**	3	0.8	**1.2**	3	1.1	**0.9**
4	2.1	(1.75)	4	0.6	(0.56)	4	0.7	(1.07)	4	0.6	(0.83)
5	1.2		5	0.8		5	0.8		5	0.9	
6	0.5		6	0.9		6	1.4		6	0.9	
7	0		7	1.2		7	1.2		7	0.4	
8	0		8	0.7		8	0.4		8	1.1	
9	0.5	**0.3**	9	1.2	**1.6**	9	1.4	**0.9**	9	2.1	**1.2**
10	0.6	(0.36)	10	1.3	(1.80)	10	0.7	(1.01)	10	1.1	(1.24)
11	0.6		11	1.8		11	1.9		11	0.9	
12	0		12	2.8		12	0		12	2.3	
13	1.1		13	1.8		13	1.0		13	1.5	
14	0		14	1.3		14	0		14	0.4	
15	1.7	**0.5**	15	1.4	**1.5**	15	0.9	**0.5**	15	2.5	**1.1**
16	0	(0)	16	0.9	(1.43)	16	0	(0.65)	16	1.4	(1.05)
17	0		17	1.7		17	0		17	0	
18	0		18	0.9		18	0		18	0	

HAYDOCK

DISTANCE 5F, 6F GOOD GROUND TO HARD		DISTANCES 5F, 6F GROUND/SOFT TO HEAVY GROUND		DISTANCE 7F 30y			DISTANCES 8F 30y, 10F 120y			DISTANCES 11F 200y, 14F, 16F 45y		
STALLS	HIGH	STALLS	HIGH	STALLS	LOW		STALLS	LOW		STALLS	LOW	
1		1		1	1.3		1	1.3		1	0.5	
2		2		2	2.8		2	0.5		2	1.4	
3		3		3	1.3	1.4	3	0.5	1.0	3	0.5	0.8
4	1.2	4	0.9	4	0	(1.4)	4	1.3	(0.99)	4	0.5	(0.79)
5		5		5	1.6		5	0.5		5	1.0	
6		6		6	0		6	1.3		6	0.6	
7		7		7	0.9		7	1.4		7	1.1	
8		8		8	0.9	0.8	8	1.1		8	2.2	1.1
9		9		9	1.3	(0.84)	9	1.0	1.1	9	0.6	(1.1)
10		10		10	0.5		10	0.7	(1.13)	10	0.5	
11		11		11	1.1		11	0.7		11	0.6	
12	0.8	12	0.7	12	0		12	1.7		12	1.5	
13		13		13	0.4	0.8	13	1.3		13	1.2	1.4
14		14		14	1.0	(0.62)	14	0.6		14	1.7	(1.23)
15		15		15	1.3		15	0		15	1.7	
16		16		16	1.6		16	1.4	0.7	16	0	
17		17					17	0	(0.6)	17	0	0.9
18		18					18	0		18	4	(1.08)
19		19					19	0		19	0	
20	0.8	20	2.6							20	0	
21		21										
22		22										
23		23										
24		24										

HAYDOCK 5F & 6F – The above data is drawn from the last two seasons only. The stalls used to be placed on the stands side but during the last two seasons they have been placed in the centre and this, as well as the increased use of watering, has resulted in the big advantage previously enjoyed by the high numbers being significantly reduced.

KEMPTON
(ROUND COURSE)

DISTANCES 5F, 6F		DISTANCES 5F, 6F		DISTANCES 7F, 8F, 9F			DISTANCES 11F 30y, 12F, 14F, 16F		
STALLS	HIGH	STALLS	LOW	STALLS	HIGH		STALLS	HIGH	
1		1		1	1.7		1	1.3	
2		2		2	1.1		2	0.9	
3	**1.7**	3	**0.8**	3	1.1	**1.1**	3	0.4	**0.8**
4	(1.46)4	4	(0.78) 4	4	0.9 (1.18)	4	4	0.4 (0.76)	
5		5		5	0.7		5	1.1	
6		6		6	0.4		6	0.8	
7		7		7	0.4		7	1.3	
8	**0.5**	8	**1.2**	8	1.5	**1.1**	8	0.6	**1.1**
9	(0.56)9	9	(1.14) 9	9	1.9 (0.95)	9	9	1.5 (1.17)	
10		10		10	1.4		10	1.1	
11		11		11	1.3		11	2.2	
12		12		12	0.4		12	1.3	
13	**0.8**	13	**1.2**	13	0.3	**0.8**	13	1.1	**1.5**
14	(0.92)14	14	(1.48) 14	14	1.1 (0.84)	14	14	1.7 (1.48)	
15		15		15	0		15	0	
16		16		16	0.4		16	0	
17		17		17	0		17	0	
18		18	**1.0**	18	0	**0.2**	18	0	**0**
19	**0.6**	19	(1.3)	19	0 (0)		19	0 (0)	
20	(0.64)20	20	20	20	20		20		
21		21					21	0	
22		22							
23		23	**1.6**						
		24	(1.6)						
		25							
		26							

KEMPTON
(JUBILEE)

DISTANCES 7F, 8F		DISTANCE 10F	
STALLS	*HIGH*	*STALLS*	*LOW*
1		1	
2		2	
3	1.2	3	1.7
4	(0.95)	4	(1.77)
5		5	
6		6	
7		7	
8	1.1	8	0.7
9	(1.23)	9	(0.7)
10		10	
11		11	
12		12	
13	0.7	13	0.5
14	(0.88)	14	(0.37)
15		15	
16		16	
17		17	
18	0.5	18	
19	(0.47)	19	0
20		20	(0)
		21	
		22	

LEICESTER

DISTANCES 5F 2y, 5F 218y, 7F 9y, 8F 8y			DISTANCES 5F 2y, 5F 218y, 7F 9y, 8F 8y			DISTANCES 9F 218y, 11F 183y		
STALLS	*HIGH*		*STALLS*	*LOW*		*STALLS*	*HIGH*	
1	1.3		1	1.2		1	1.1	
2	1.0		2	0.7		2	0.3	
3	0.3	**0.8**	3	1.6	**1.0**	3	0.5	**0.9**
4	1.3		4	0.5	(0.9)	4	1.4	(0.91)
5	0.3		5	0.9		5	0.9	
6	1.3		6	1.0		6	0.5	
7	1.3		7	0.9		7	1.4	
8	0.6	**1.1**	8	0.9	**1.1**	8	0.9	**1.0**
9	0.7		9	1.4	(1.14)	9	1.4	(0.96)
10	1.5		10	1.4		10	0.5	
11	1.2		11	0.3		11	0.9	
12	1.3		12	0.4		12	1.1	
13	1.6	**1.4**	13	1.1	**0.9**	13	1.5	**1.2**
14	1.2		14	2.4	(0.99)	14	1.5	(1.19)
15	1.6		15	0.4		15	1.3	
16	2.0		16	0.9		16	2.2	
17	0		17	1.4		17	0.9	**1.0**
18	0		18	0.6		18	0	(0.97)
19	1.3	**0.9**	19	1.0	**0.9**	19	0	
20	1.8		20	0	(0.89)			
21	0		21	0				
22	0		22	0				

LINGFIELD

(TURF)

DISTANCES 5F, 6F			DISTANCES 5F, 6F		DISTANCES 7F, 7F 140y			DISTANCES 9F, 10F, 11F 106y		
STALLS	HIGH		STALLS	LOW	STALLS	HIGH		STALLS	LOW	
1	0.8		1		1	1.4		1	1.4	
2	1.8		2		2	0.6		2	1.3	**1.3**
3	1.5	**1.5**	3	0.9	3	1.8	**1.3**	3	1.7	(1.52)
4	2.2	(1.47)	4		4	1.5	(1.23)	4	0.9	
5	1.0		5		5	1.1		5	1.0	
6	0.4		6		6	1.3		6	1.2	**1.1**
7	0.8		7		7	1.6		7	1.0	(1.04)
8	0.7	**0.7**	8	0.6	8	0.6		8	1.3	
9	0.7	(0.67)	9		9	1.0	**0.9**	9	0.3	
10	1.1		10		10	0.3	(0.97)	10	0.5	**0.5**
11	1.1		11		11	1.0		11	0.8	(0.42)
12	0		12		12	0.8		12	0.8	
13	0.9	**0.6**	13	1.6	13	0.6		13	0	
14	0	(0.57)	14		14	0		14	0	
15	0.8		15		15	0.3		15	1.2	
16	1.1		16		16	0.6	**0.5**	16	0	**0.2**
17	0		17		17	0.9	(0.49)	17	0	(0)
18	1.9	**0.8**	18	1.4	18	3.0		18	0	
19	0	(0.96)	19		19	0		19	0	
20	0		20		20	0		20	0	

LINGFIELD 5F & 6F – Beware of watering! Whenever the ground has been watered the advantage held by the high numbers is usually reduced or nullified.

MUSSELBURGH

DISTANCE 5F		DISTANCE 5F		DISTANCES 7F, 8F		DISTANCE 9F		DISTANCES 12F, 13F, 14F	
STALLS	*HIGH*	*STALLS*	*LOW*	*STALLS*	*HIGH*	*STALLS*	*HIGH*	*STALLS*	*HIGH*
1	0.7	1	1.4	1	1.7	1		1	
2	0 **0.9**	2	1.3 **1.2**	2	0.7	2		2	**0.9**
3	0.7 (0.88)	3	0.8 (1.04)	3	1.1 **1.2**	3	**1.1**	3	(0.96)
4	2.1	4	0	4	1.5 (1.14)	4		4	
5	0	5	2.2	5	1.1	5		5	
6	2.1 **1.1**	6	1.4	6	0.3	6		6	**1.2**
7	0.7 (1.06)	7	0.6	7	2.0	7		7	(1.17)
8	1.4	8	0.8 **0.9**	8	0.8 **0.8**	8		8	
9	0.8	9	1.5 (0.94)	9	0.5 (0.78)	9	**1.2**	9	
10	0.8 **1.2**	10	0.2	10	0.5	10		10	**0.6**
11	1.8 (1.17)	11	1.3	11	0.5	11		11	(0.43)
12	1.2	12	0	12	1.1	12		12	
13	1.4	13	1.9	13	1.1 **0.9**	13		13	
14	0	14	0 **1.0**	14	0.6 (1.03)	14	0	14	**2.0**
15	1.8 **1.1**	15	0 (1.1)	15	0	15		15	(2.50)
16	1.9	16	2.8	16	0	16		16	
17	0	17	4.2			17			

NEWBURY

DISTANCES 5F 34y, 6F 8y, 7F, 8F (STRAIGHT COURSE)

STALLS	HIGH	
1	1.7	
2	1.4	
3	1.0	**1.1**
4	0.3	(1.25)
5	1.4	
6	0.9	
7	0.9	
8	0.9	**0.9**
9	0.9	(0.81)
10	0.7	
11	0.9	
12	0.8	
13	0.5	**0.9**
14	0.9	(0.78)
15	1.5	
16	0.7	
17	1.0	
18	1.1	**1.1**
19	2.2	(1.1)
20	3.7	
21	0	
22	0	
23	2.5	**1.7**
24	4	(1.4)
25 - 28	0	

DISTANCES 7F 64y, 8F (ROUND COURSE) GOOD GROUND TO HARD GROUND

STALLS	LOW	
1	1.4	
2	0.9	
3	1.8	**1.4**
4	1.4	
5	1.4	
6	1.8	
7	0.5	
8	1.4	**1.1**
9	1.7	
10	0	
11	0	
12	0	
13	0	**0.2**
14	1.4	
15	0	
16	0	
17	0	
18	0	**0**
19	0	
20	0	

DISTANCES 7F 64y, 8F (ROUND COURSE) GOOD/SOFT TO HEAVY GROUND

STALLS	LOW
1	
2	
3	**0.3**
4	
5	
6	
7	
8	**1.0**
9	
10	
11	
12	
13	**2.0**
14	
15	
16	
17	
18	**1.4**
19	
20	

DISTANCES 9F, 10F, 11F 12F, 13F GOOD/SOFT GROUND TO HARD

STALLS	LOW	
1	1.0	
2	1.5	
3	0.8	**1.1**
4	1.1	(1.15)
5	0.8	
6	0.6	
7	1.1	
8	0.4	**0.9**
9	1.2	(0.75)
10	1.3	
11	1.0	
12	1.4	
13	0	**1.0**
14	2.3	(0.88)
15	0	
16	1.0	
17	3.7	
18	0	
19	0	**1.4**
20	1.7	(1.75)
21	2.1	
22	0	

DISTANCES 9F, 10F, 11F 12F, 13F SOFT GROUND TO HEAVY

STALLS	LOW
1	
2	
3	
4	**0.9**
5	(0.75)
6	
7	
8	
9	
10	
11	**0.8**
12	(1.0)
13	
14	
15	
16	
17	
18	**3.1**
19	(3.17)
20	
21	
22	

NEWCASTLE

DISTANCES 5F, 6F, 7F, 8F 3y (STRAIGHT COURSE)			DISTANCES 8F, 9F, 10F 32y (ROUND COURSE)			DISTANCES 12F 93y, 14F, 16F		
STALLS	HIGH		STALLS	LOW		STALLS	LOW	
1	1.4		1	0.4		1	0.5	
2	1.6		2	1.3		2	1.2	
3	1.3	**1.1**	3	1.4	**1.3**	3	1.7	**1.1**
4	0.6	(1.12)	4	1.3	(1.44)	4	1.4	(1.13)
5	0.6		5	2.3		5	0.8	
6	1.1		6	1.1		6	1.3	
7	0.5		7	0.7		7	0.9	
8	0.6	**0.8**	8	0.7	**0.9**	8	0.6	**0.8**
9	1.0	(0.78)	9	0.9	(0.85)	9	0.7	(0.81)
10	0.9		10	1.4		10	0.4	
11	1.0		11	0.7		11	1.6	
12	0.7		12	1.2		12	1.2	
13	0.8	**0.8**	13	0.8	**0.7**	13	0.9	**1.2**
14	0.3	(0.8)	14	0.2	(0.73)	14	1.8	(1.33)
15	1.2		15	0.6		15	0	
16	2.9		16	0		16	0	
17	2.0		17	0		17	1.25	
18	0	**1.7**	18	0.5		18	0	**0.4**
19	1.4	(1.79)	19	0	**0.2**	19	0	(0)
20	2.1		20	0	(0)	20	0	
			21	0				
			22	0				

NEWCASTLE (STRAIGHT COURSE) – Although not a hard and fast rule the advantage held by the low numbers in big fields is greatest when the ground is between good/soft and heavy.

NEWMARKET

(JULY)

DISTANCES 5F, 6F, 7F, 8F			DISTANCES 5F, 6F, 7F, 8F			DISTANCES 10F, 12F		
STALLS	HIGH		STALLS	LOW		STALLS	HIGH	
1	1.6		1	0.3		1	1.4	
2	2.0		2	0.6		2	0.9	
3	1.1	**1.2**	3	1.5	**0.9**	3	0.8	**1.2**
4	0.4	(1.15)	4	1.5	(0.85)	4	1.4	(1.02)
5	0.9		5	0.6		5	1.0	
6	1.3		6	1.3		6	1.4	
7	0.7		7	1.5		7	1.6	
8	1.3	**1.2**	8	1.1	**1.0**	8	0.7	**1.2**
9	1.7	(1.27)	9	0.7	(1.12)	9	1.2	(1.24)
10	0.7		10	0.6		10	1.1	
11	0.8		11	1.6		11	0	
12	0.9		12	0.8		12	0.4	
13	0.4	**0.6**	13	0.2	**1.0**	13	1.1	**0.5**
14	0	(0.45)	14	1.4	(0.96)	14	0.9	(0.58)
15	0.6		15	0.7		15	0	
16	0.8		16	0.4		16	0	
17	0		17	2.1		17	0	
18	0	**0.5**	18	1.4		18	0	**0.6**
19	1.7	(0.62)	19	1.7	**1.2**	19	0	(0.69)
20	0		20	0	(1.33)	20	3.3	
			21	0		21	0	
			22	0		22	0	
						23	0	
						24	0	**0**
						25	0	(0)
						26	0	
						27	0	
						28 +	0	

NEWMARKET
(ROWLEY)

DISTANCES 5F, 6F, 7F		DISTANCES 8F, 9F, 10F		DISTANCES 12F, 14F, 16F	
STALLS	HIGH	STALLS	HIGH	STALLS	HIGH
1	2.0	1		1	
2	1.8	2		2	
3	1.4 **1.3**	3	**1.2**	3	**1.4**
4	0.4 (1.5)	4	(1.2)	4	(1.43)
5	1.2	5		5	
6	0.2	6		6	
7	0.4	7		7	
8	1.9 **0.8**	8	**1.0**	8	**0.8**
9	0.4 (0.62)	9	(0.96)	9	(0.64)
10	1.1	10		10	
11	0	11		11	
12	0.5	12		12	
13	0.6 **0.8**	13	**1.0**	13	**0.3**
14	0.6 (0.89)	14	(0.96)	14	(0.42)
15	2.4	15		15	
16	1.6	16		16	
17	1.9	17		17	
18	0.9 **1.2**	18	**1.0**	18	**0.2**
19	1.1 (1.28)	19	(1.25)	19	(0.29)
20	0	20		20	
21	0.4	21		21	
22	0.7	22		22	
23	0.8	23		23	
24	0 **0.9**	24	**0.8**	24	**0.6**
25	0.8 (0.5)	25	(0.66)	25	(0.39)
26	0.8	26		26	
27	4	27		27	
28 +	0	28 +		28 +	

NOTTINGHAM

DISTANCES 5F 13y, 6F 15y		DISTANCES 8F 54y, 9F 213y			DISTANCES 14F 15y, 16F 9y		
STALLS	HIGH	STALLS	LOW		STALLS	LOW	
1		1	0.6		1	1.1	
2		2	1.1		2	1.0	
3	1.1	3	1.1	1.0	3	0.4	0.9
4		4	1.6	(1.03)	4	1.4	(0.89)
5		5	1.1		5	0.2	
6		6	0.8		6	1.3	
7		7	0.8		7	2.2	
8	1.1	8	0.8		8	1.0	
9		9	0.9	0.9	9	0.9	1.2
10		10	0.5	(0.88)	10	0.7	(1.21)
11		11	1.5		11	0.7	
12		12	1.1		12	1.4	
13	0.6	13	1.2		13	0.8	
14		14	0.6		14	0.4	
15		15	1.1	1.0	15	1.2	0.8
16		16	0.7	(1.17)	16	2.2	(0.82)
17		17	1.7		17	0	
18	1.1	18	1.4		18	0	
19							
20							

PONTEFRACT

DISTANCES 5F, 6F GOOD GROUND TO HARD GROUND			DISTANCES 5F, 6F GOOD/SOFT TO HEAVY GROUND			DISTANCE 8F 4y			DISTANCES 10F 6y, 12F 8y		
STALLS	LOW		STALLS	LOW		STALLS	LOW		STALLS	LOW	
1	0		1	0.8		1	2.2		1	1.6	
2	0.3		2	1.7		2	0.5		2	0.8	
3	1.5	**0.9**	3	0	**0.9**	3	0.4	**1.2**	3	1.4	**1.2**
4	1.7	(0.95)	4	2.0	(0.87)	4	0.3	(1.08)	4	1.3	(1.06)
5	1.4		5	0		5	2.5		5	0.6	
6	0.9		6	0.8		6	0.9		6	1.3	
7	0.9		7	0		7	0.8		7	1.2	
8	1.7		8	2.0		8	0.7	**0.9**	8	0.6	**1.0**
9	0.3	**1.4**	9	0.8	**0.9**	9	1.2	(0.81)	9	0.9	(1.02)
10	1.8	(1.36)	10	1.9	(0.92)	10	0.8		10	1.3	
11	2.4		11	0		11	1.3		11	1.7	
12	1.5		12	0.9		12	0.4		12	0.5	
13	0		13	0		13	0.6	**0.9**	13	0.6	**0.9**
14	1.7		14	1.2		14	1.4	(0.88)	14	0.7	(0.95)
15	0	**0.7**	15	0	**1.6**	15	0.9		15	0.8	
16	2.2	(0.83)	16	4	(1.80)	16	0.9		16	1.0	
17	0		17	2		17	1.1		17	0	**0.2**
18	0		18	4		18	2.4	**1.3**	18	0	(0.30)
						19	0	(1.60)	19	0	
						20	4				

REDCAR

STALLS	HIGH		STALLS	LOW		STALLS	LOW	
	DISTANCES 5F, 6F, 7F, 8F			**DISTANCES 9F, 10F, 11F**			**DISTANCES 13.5F, 14F, 16F**	
1	0.9		1	0.2		1	1.2	
2	0.6		2	0.8		2	1.5	**1.2**
3	0.6	**0.9**	3	1.0	**0.9**	3	1.0	(1.46)
4	1.3	(0.93)	4	2.0	(0.86)	4	1.0	
5	1.3		5	1.2		5	0.7	
6	1.3		6	0.4		6	1.2	**1.1**
7	1.4		7	1.0		7	1.6	(1.0)
8	1.3	**1.2**	8	1.0		8	0.7	
9	0.8	(1.29)	9	1.1	**1.0**	9	0.3	
10	1.4		10	1.9	(1.08)	10	0.4	**0.7**
11	1.3		11	0.2		11	2.4	(0.41)
12	0.6		12	0.8		12	0	
13	1.4	**0.9**	13	0.9		13	0.5	
14	1.1	(0.85)	14	1.5		14	0.9	**0.4**
15	0.4		15	1.0	**1.3**	15	0	(0.37)
16	0.5		16	1.9	(1.31)	16	0	
17	1.1		17	2.0				
18	0.3	**0.6**						
19	0	(0.64)						
20	1.2							
21	1.8							
22	1.2							
23	0							
24	0.6	**1.2**						
25	1.9	(1.27)						
26	3.1							
27	0							
28	0.3							

RIPON

DISTANCES 5F, 6F

STALLS	LOW	
1	1.4	
2	1.2	
3	1.0	**1.1**
4	1.2	(1.15)
5	0.9	
6	1.2	
7	0.2	
8	0.7	
9	1.0	**0.6**
10	0.3	(0.58)
11	0	
12	1.2	
13	1.5	
14	0	
15	0.5	**0.8**
16	0.5	(0.66)
17	1.2	
18	0.5	
19	4.3	
20	2.1	
21	2.9	**3.1**
22	3.1	(3.27)
23	1.5	

DISTANCES 8F, 9F

STALLS	HIGH	
1	1.5	
2	1.2	
3	1.1	**1.0**
4	0.8	(0.99)
5	0.3	
6	1.1	
7	0.8	
8	1.1	**1.1**
9	2.4	(1.04)
10	0	
11	1.1	
12	0	
13	0.8	**0.9**
14	3.0	(0.95)
15	1.0	
16	0	
17	0	
18	2.2	**0.5**
19	0	(0.58)
20	0	

DISTANCES 10F, 12F 60y

STALLS	HIGH	
1	0.9	
2	1.8	
3	1.7	**1.3**
4	0.8	(1.24)
5	1.1	
6	0.3	
7	1.2	
8	0.5	**0.8**
9	1.0	(0.74)
10	0.7	
11	0.3	
12	0.4	
13	0.6	**0.9**
14	0.8	(1.08)
15	3.6	
16	0	
17	1.4	
18	0	
19	0	
20	0	**0.6**
21	0	(0.74)
22	0	
23	4	
24	0	
25	0	

RIPON 5F & 6F – When the course has been watered, the bias in favour of stalls 19-23 is lessened or nullified and the middle draws come into the reckoning

SALISBURY

DISTANCES 5F, 6F			DISTANCES 5F, 6F		DISTANCES 6F 212y, 8F			DISTANCES 9F 198y, 12F, 14F 15y		
STALLS	HIGH		STALLS	LOW	STALLS	HIGH		STALLS	HIGH	
1	2.0		1		1	1.4		1	1.4	
2	1.3		2		2	0.9		2	1.3	
3	1.6	1.4	3	0.5	3	2.1	1.4	3	0.9	1.0
4	1.0	(1.29)	4	(0.51)	4	1.7	(1.2)	4	0.7	(0.9)
5	1.0		5		5	0.9		5	0.5	
6	0		6		6	0.9		6	1.3	
7	0.3		7		7	1.0		7	1.1	
8	0.3	0.6	8	1.3	8	0.7	1.0	8	1.0	1.2
9	1.5	(0.6)	9	(1.34)	9	1.0	(1.11)	9	1.4	(1.36)
10	1.3		10		10	1.4		10	1.4	
11	0.5		11		11	1.6		11	0.9	
12	1.0		12		12	0.8		12	0.7	
13	0.6	1.0	13	1.1	13	0.5	0.7	13	0	0.76
14	1.9	(1.18)	14	(1.1)	14	0	(0.75)	14	0.5	(0.68)
15	2.7		15		15	0		15	2.1	
16	0		16		16	0.7		16	0	
17	2.4		17		17	0		17	1.2	
18	0	0.7	18	0	18	0	0.2	18	0	0.7
19	0	(0.88)	19	(0)	19	0	(0.27)	19	0	(0.44)
20	0		20		20	0		20	4	

SANDOWN

DISTANCE 5F		DISTANCE 5F		DISTANCES 9F, 10F 7y, 11F 91y		DISTANCES 7F16y, 8F14y GOOD GROUND TO HARD GROUND		DISTANCES 7F16y, 8F14y, GOOD/SOFT GROUND TO HEAVY GROUND	
STALLS	HIGH	STALLS	LOW	STALLS	HIGH	STALLS	HIGH	STALLS	HIGH
1	1.6	1		1	1.5	1	1.1	1	0.4
2	1.8 **1.4**	2	**0.6**	2	1.5	2	0.5	2	1.6
3	0.8 (1.3)	3	(0.59)	3	1.0 **1.2**	3	1.3 **1.3**	3	1.6 **0.9**
4	1.3	4		4	1.3 (1.24)	4	1.9 (1.47)	4	0 (0.88)
5	0.8	5		5	0.8	5	1.6	5	0.8
6	1.0 **1.2**	6	**1.2**	6	1.0	6	1.3	6	1.1
7	1.6 (1.22)	7	(1.19)	7	0.8	7	0.6	7	0.4
8	1.6	8		8	0.8 **0.9**	8	0.3	8	1.1
9	0.3	9		9	1.2 (0.9)	9	1.0 **0.6**	9	1.8 **1.0**
10	1.0 **0.4**	10		10	0.4	10	0.8 (0.63)	10	0.5 (1.07)
11	0 (0.52)	11	**1.2**	11	0.4	11	1.1	11	0
12	0	12	(1.23)	12	0.6	12	0.6	12	1.9
13	1.4	13		13	0 **0.9**	13	0.8	13	2.6
14	1.7			14	2.6 (0.79)	14	1.4	14	0
15	0			15	2.2	15	0 **0.9**	15	0 **1.0**
16	0 **0.9**			16	0	16	1.5 (0.69)	16	0 (0.96)
17	0 (0.71)			17	0	17	0	17	0
18	0			18	0 **0.5**	18	0	18	0
19	0			19	2.3 (0.53)				
				20	0				

THIRSK

DISTANCES 5F, 6F			DISTANCES 7F, 8F			DISTANCES 12F +		
STALLS	HIGH		STALLS	LOW		STALLS	LOW	
1	1.8		1	1.2		1		
2	2.5		2	0.7		2		
3	2.4	**1.7**	3	0.7	**1.2**	3	**1.1**	
4	0.7	(1.56)	4	1.0	(1.29)	4	(1.21)	
5	1.3		5	2.2		5		
6	1.2		6	1.8		6		
7	1.1		7	0.9		7		
8	0.7		8	1.3		8		
9	0.8	**0.3**	9	0.6	**0.8**	9	**1.0**	
10	0	(0.35)	10	0.7	(0.64)	10	(0.9)	
11	0.5		11	0.3		11		
12	0.3		12	0.9		12		
13	0.7		13	1.2		13		
14	0.4		14	0.7		14		
15	0.9	**0.5**	15	0.7	**0.8**	15	**1.1**	
16	0	(0.51)	16	0.5	(1.0)	16	(1.12)	
17	0.4		17	0		17		
18	0.9		18	1.8		18		
19	0							
20	2.2							
21	0	**0.7**						
22	0	(0.9)						
23	2.8							
24	0							

WARWICK

DISTANCES 5F GOOD GROUND TO HARD		DISTANCES 6F, 7F, 8F GOOD GROUND TO HARD GROUND			DISTANCES 6F, 7F, 8F GOOD/SOFT GROUND TO HEAVY GROUND			DISTANCES 10F 169y			DISTANCES 12F, 16F	
STALLS	LOW	STALLS	LOW		STALLS	LOW		STALLS	LOW		STALLS	LOW
1		1	1.4		1	0.9		1	1.9		1	
2		2	2.2	**1.4**	2	0.8		2	1.0	**1.1**	2	
3	**1.8**	3	2.2	(1.44)	3	0.5	**0.7**	3	1.0	(1.2)	3	**1.3**
4	(1.86)	4	0		4	0.9	(0.54)	4	0.3		4	(1.26)
5		5	0.5		5	0.5		5	0.7		5	
6		6	1.6	**1.0**	6	0.8		6	0.7	**1.1**	6	
7		7	0.8	(0.94)	7	2.7		7	1.4	(1.12)	7	
8	**0.5**	8	1.1		8	2.4		8	1.6		8	
9	(0.26)	9	0.3		9	0.6	**1.2**	9	0.5		9	**0.5**
10		10	2.2	**0.9**	10	0	(1.17)	10	0.5	**0.7**	10	(0.44)
11		11	0.9	(0.93)	11	0.6		11	1.6	(0.6)	11	
12		12	0.5		12	0.6		12	0		12	
13	**0.7**	13	0		13	1.5		13	0		13	
14	(0.72)	14	0		14	0		14	1.8	**(0.4)**	13	
15		15	0		15	0.8		15	0	(0.53)	15	
16		16	0	**0.2**	16	3.2	**0.8**	16	0		16	**0.9**
17		17	0	(0.17)	17	0	(0.89)	17	2.8		17	(0.9)
18	**0.7**	18	1.3		18	0		18	3.1	**1.9**	18	
19	(0.72)	19	0		19	0		19	0	(1.76)	19	
20		20	0		20	0		20	0		20	

WARWICK 6F, 7F, 8F (GOOD/SOFT TO HEAVY) – The softer the ground the bigger the advantage enjoyed by the high numbers. The lowest six stalls have a poor record compared to when the ground is riding fast.

WINDSOR

DISTANCES 5F 10y, 6F GOOD GROUND TO HARD GROUND			DISTANCES 5F 10y, 6F GOOD/SOFT GROUND TO HEAVY GROUND		DISTANCE 8F 67y			DISTANCES 10F 7y, 11F 135y		
STALLS	HIGH		STALLS	HIGH	STALLS	HIGH		STALLS	HIGH	
1	1.8		1		1	0.9		1	1.3	
2	1.8	**1.3**	2	**1.6**	2	1.1	**1.3**	2	1.1	**1.1**
3	1.8	(1.21)	3	(1.25)	3	1.4	(1.19)	3	0.9	(1.13)
4	0		4		4	1.8		4	1.0	
5	2.2		5		5	1.8		5	1.7	
6	0.5	**1.3**	6	**1.1**	6	0.9	**1.2**	6	0.7	**1.2**
7	1.2	(1.37)	7	(1.25)	7	1.2	(1.05)	7	1.2	(1.25)
8	1.3		8		8	1.0		8	1.0	
9	0.5		9		9	1.2		9	0.4	
10	0.5	**0.6**	10	**0.6**	10	1.3	**0.8**	10	0.6	**0.8**
11	0.3	(0.49)	11	(0.64)	11	0.3	(1.04)	11	1.1	(0.69)
12	1.1		12		12	0.3		12	0.6	
13	0.4		13		13	1.1		13	0.5	
14	0	**0.7**	14	**0.4**	14	0		14	0.7	
15	1.9	(0.78)	15	(0.46)	15	0.9	**0.4**	15	1.9	
16	0.6		16		16	0	(0.56)	16	0	
17	2.6		17		17	0		17	4.0	**1.0**
18	0		18	**0.4**	18	0		18	0	(0.78)
19	0		19	(0.51)				19	0	
20	0		20					20	2.0	
21	0	**0.6**	21					21	0	
22	0	(0.76)	22							
23	0		23	**1.8**						
24	0		24	(2.11)						
25	0		25							

WINDSOR 5F 10y & 6F (GOOD/SOFT TO HEAVY) – In big fields the runners who race against the far rail often have a significant advantage, but this was not apparent during 2001.

YARMOUTH

DISTANCES 5F 43y, 6F 3y, 7F 3y, 8F 3y			DISTANCES 5F 43y, 6F 3y, 7F 3y, 8F 3y			DISTANCES 10F 21y, 11F 101y		
STALLS	HIGH		STALLS	LOW		STALLS	LOW	
1	1.6		1	1.0		1	0.4	
2	1.7		2	1.2		2	1.3	
3	1.1	**1.3**	3	0.6	**1.0**	3	1.1	**1.1**
4	0.8	(1.37)	4	1.2	(0.9)	4	1.1	(1.26)
5	1.5		5	0.8		5	1.5	
6	1.3		6	1.2		6	0.4	
7	0.9		7	1.2		7	0.9	
8	0.3	**0.8**	8	0.6	**1.1**	8	1.2	**0.9**
9	0.6	(0.77)	9	1.0	(1.15)	9	1.0	(0.83)
10	0.8		10	1.8		10	1.0	
11	0.3		11	1.7		11	0.9	
12	0.4		12	1.6		12	0.4	
13	0.5	**0.6**	13	0.9	**1.0**	13	0.8	**0.9**
14	2.4	(0.43)	14	0	(1.05)	14	1.5	(0.73)
15	0		15	0		15	1.3	
16	0		16	0		16	2.7	
17	1.0		17	1.6		17	0	
18	2.9	**1.2**	18	2.2	**1.0**	18	0	**1.5**
19	0	(1.2)	19	1.0	(1.0)	19	0	(0.73)
20	4		20	0		20	0	

YARMOUTH (STRAIGHT COURSE, HIGH) – The low numbers do best in fields of 17- 20 runners when the ground is riding between good/soft and heavy. The middle draws are at a big disadvantage on soft ground in big fields.

YORK

DISTANCES 5F, 6F

STALLS	HIGH		
1	0.6		
2	0.3		
3	0	0.4	(0.41)
4	0.7		
5	1.5		
6	0.7	1.3	(1.22)
7	1.0		
8	1.7		
9	1.3		
10	0.3	0.8	(0.81)
11	1.2		
12	0.3		
13	1.6		
14	1.3	1.8	(1.82)
15	2.3		
16	2.3		
17	0		
18	4.3	1.6	(1.62)
19	1.8		
20	0.5		
21	0		
22	0		
23	0	0	(0)
24	0		
25	0		
26	0		

DISTANCES 5F, 6F

STALLS	LOW		
1			
2	1.5		
3			(1.53)
4			
5			
6	0.5		
7			(0.51)
8			
9			
10	1.0		
11			(1.02)
12			
13			
14	2.1		
15			(2.14)
16			
17			
18	0.8		
19			(0.83)
20			
21			
22	0		
23			(0)

DISTANCE 6F 214y

STALLS	HIGH		
1			
2	1.1		
3			(0.95)
4			
5			
6	1.5		
7			(1.58)
8			
9			
10	0		
11			(0)
12			
13			
14	2.3		
15			(2.46)
16			
17			
18	0.8		
19			(0.88)
20			
21			
22	0		
23			(0)

DISTANCE 6F 214y

STALLS	LOW		
1			
2	0.8		
3			(0.59)
4			
5			
6	1.4		
7			(1.19)
8			
9			
10	0		
11			(0)
12			
13			
14	2.3		
15			(2.63)
16			
17			
18	1.5		
19			(1.72)
20			
21			
22	0		
23			(0)

DISTANCES 7F 202y, 8F 205y

STALLS	LOW		
1	1.8		
2	2.5		
3	1.8	1.7	(1.93)
4	0.7		
5	0.7		
6	0.4		
7	1.4	1.2	(0.91)
8	2.1		
9	1.1		
10	0.8		
11	0	0.8	(0.78)
12	0		
13	0		
14	0		
15	0	0.2	(0.21)
16	0.8		
17	1.1		
18	0		
19	0	0.3	(0.42)
20	0		
21	0		
22	0		
23	3.2		
24	0		
25	0	0.3	(0.4)
26	0		

DISTANCES 10F 85y, 11F 195y

STALLS	LOW		
1	1.4		
2	2.7	1.4	(1.64)
3	0.8		
4	0.8		
5	0.8		
6	1.1	1.1	(1.12)
7	0.8		
8	1.8		
9	0		
10	2.2	0.9	(0.72)
11	1.3		
12	0		
13	0.4		
14	1.4	0.6	(0.47)
15	0		
16	0.5		
17	0		
18	0		
19	0.6	0.4	(0.28)
20	1.5		
21	0		
22	0		

DISTANCE 13F 194y

STALLS	LOW		
1			
2	2.0		
3			(1.52)
4			
5			
6	1.0		
7			(1.05)
8			
9			
10	0.4		
11			(0.52)
12			
13			
14	0.4		
15			(0.5)
16			
17			
18			
19	0.6		
20			(0.4)
21			
22			